Hunting for Hides

Hunting for Hides

Deerskins, Status, and Cultural Change in the Protohistoric Appalachians

Heather A. Lapham

THE UNIVERSITY OF ALABAMA PRESS

Tuscaloosa

Typeface: AGaramond

Cover illustration: *Hunting Deer,* De Bry engraving
#25, 1591, after Le Moyne, 1564
Cover design: Erin Bradley Dangar / Dangar Design

Cataloging-in-Publication Data is available from
the Library of Congress

ISBN-13: 978-0-8173-1493-4 (cloth)

ISBN-13: 978-0-8173-5276-9 (paper)

E-ISBN-13: 978-0-8173-8377-0 (electronic)

Contents

Figures

Tables

Acknowledgments

This book represents a revision of my dissertation, which I completed in May 2002 at the University of Virginia. I had the good fortune of having my dissertation research and writing supported by a Predoctoral Fellowship at the National Museum of Natural History, Smithsonian Institution, and a Pollard Dissertation Fellowship from the University of Virginia. A Graduate Fellowship from the Virginia Museum of Natural History provided initial funding to study the faunal remains from several features at the Hoge site.

I find it difficult to put into words the gratitude I feel for all of the support I have received over the years. Brevity, I believe, is the most sincere approach I can take in expressing my appreciation. Many thanks go to my dissertation committee for their thoughtful insights, constructive criticisms, and excellent guidance: Jeffrey Hantman, John Shepherd, Bruce Smith, Patricia Wattenmaker, and Melinda Zeder. This research project came about from conversations with Jeff, and his assistance along the way has been greatly appreciated. Pati has given me instrumental advice on all aspects of my research, and John, with his exceptional eye for details, provided essential feedback on my dissertation.

I am especially grateful to Bruce who, many years ago when I was an undergraduate intern, gave me the task of counting and weighing fragments of broken ceramic cooking cones from the Middle Mississippian Snodgrass site. It was an exceptionally dusty job, but one that began my lengthy residence in the Archaeobiology Program Laboratory at the National Museum of Natural History where, in April 2002, I sat and typed the final words to my dissertation. Mindy, most of all, has been, and continues to be, an invaluable mentor and friend. Her keen advice and encouraging words will be forever remembered.

Over the years I have benefited greatly from many discussions with friends and colleagues, especially Virginia Busby, Garrett Fesler, and Seth Mallios. I also extend my thanks to Meg Hiers and Adrienne Reese for the many hours they spent with me in the Archaeobiology Laboratory sorting and identifying animal bones. Keith Egloff at the Virginia Department of Historic Resources assisted me on numerous occasions and kindly provided access to their collections, which are the foundation of my research. In addition, Keith provided the images of ceramic artifacts from the Crab Orchard and Trigg sites that I have reproduced in Chapter 2. Thanks also to Michael B. Barber, who was particularly generous with his unpublished data on the bone tools from the Trigg site; to Thomas Klatka, who graciously allowed me to use the newly returned radiocarbon dates from the Trigg site in this book; and to Matt Knox, from the Virginia Department of Game and Inland Fisheries Wildlife Division, for providing the data on modern deer harvests.

I also thank two anonymous reviewers for their comments and criticisms, all of which greatly strengthened this manuscript. Brian Butler and Paul Welch extended the occasional, and well-directed, prod to keep me focused on the transition from dissertation to book. Donna Butler and Carol Jackson gave me their support and, most importantly, their friendship throughout the revision process.

Many friends and family, especially my stepfather Ernst Kohlstruk, have been there for me over the years. They have given me the incentive to keep moving forward, even when I faltered. I am forever grateful for their support. Most of all, I thank my mom, Nancy L. Kohlstruk, who has never wavered in her belief in me and my dreams. Her strength and prayers have been a guiding force for me. She is my hero, always. It is with great love that I dedicate this book to my daddy, Davis M. Lapham, who I know is so very proud, and to the other angels who watch over me.

Hunting for Hides

1 Economic Intensification and Cultural Change

Introduction

Native American societies throughout eastern North America experienced profound cultural change during the sixteenth and seventeenth centuries due in part to the broad-reaching effects of European contact. Although a European presence in the region certainly influenced historic-era economic and sociopolitical environments, Native American peoples continued to make life choices that reflected conscious decisions about how to live in the world. If anything has become apparent from the recent resurgence of culture contact studies it is that no one coherent theory or model can adequately explain what motivated Native Americans' responses to European contact at all times and places (e.g., Cusick 1998; Fitzhugh 1985; Hudson and Tesser 1994; Rogers and Wilson 1993; Wesson and Rees 2002). Native Americans' experiences and interactions with Europeans were formed from regionally varied cultural, ecological, and historical factors. Colonial endeavors did not inevitably induce change in Native American cultural systems, nor did European powers preside over Native American polities as the agents responsible for historical developments. As Richard White has aptly stated, "Contact was not a battle of primal forces in which only one could survive. Something new could appear" (1991:ix). It is a desire to understand the "something new" that guides and inspires my research. How did historic era dynamics create new alternatives for cultural change in Native North American societies? What choices did Native Americans make in response to European contact? And, how did these choices influence cultural developments in the historic period?

Archaeologists are in a unique position to examine cultural change, as well as continuity, because archaeological data can bridge human behavior and cultural processes from the prehistoric past to the present day (Lightfoot 1995:200). Comparative studies appropriately grounded in late prehistoric Native American lifeways provide an essential foundation needed to evaluate what, how, and why particular aspects of indigenous cultural systems changed following European expansion into the Americas. To gain a more comprehensive understanding of historic-era cultural change in one region and time in eastern North America, I investigate the use of deer, deerskins, and nonlocal goods among late Late Woodland (ca. A.D. 1400–1600) and Protohistoric (ca. A.D. 1600–1700) Native American societies in the Appalachian Highlands of southwestern Virginia. In the seventeenth century, hunting deer to obtain hides for commercial trade evolved into a substantial economic enterprise for many Native Americans in the Middle Atlantic and Southeast. An overseas market demand for animal hides and furs imported from the Americas, combined with the desire of infant New World colonies to find profitable export commodities, provided a new market for processed deerskins as well as new sources of valued nonlocal goods. Understanding what motivated deer procurement and hide production for commercial trade versus local consumption and how the nonlocal goods acquired in exchange for deerskins were used is central to understanding Native American cultural change as situated within the broader context of European contact.

In this study I integrate the analyses of two often-distinct artifact categories, zooarchaeological materials and mortuary assemblages. This approach enables me to examine both the products Native Americans produced for trade (deerskins and other furs) as well as the items received in return (European-manufactured and nonlocal native-made goods). I consider animal remains to gain insights into subsistence practices, deer hunting strategies, and deerskin production activities. Using these data I investigate the following questions: To what intensity were deer exploited and hides processed in the Late Woodland period prior to the development of a commercial trade in deerskins? What evidence exists in the Protohistoric period of deerskin production for trade? And, who produced hides for this trade? My examination of the mortuary assemblages contributes information on the use of the nonlocal goods acquired through this interregional trade in deerskins. How were the nonlocal goods used? Who used these goods? And, who, if anyone, controlled their use? Considered together, these data enable me to evaluate change and continuity in Protohistoric Native American economic organization and sociopolitical systems in the southern Appalachian Highlands during the initial decades following permanent English settlement in coastal Virginia.

In the remainder of this chapter, I first consider anthropological models of economic intensification that inform my perspective on the possible factors that motivated Native American participation in the deerskin trade. Drawing on documentation regarding seventeenth- and eighteenth-century colonial markets and information on white-tailed deer bioecology, I then propose some general expectations regarding the possible ways in which this new commercial trade in deerskins may have influenced Native American economic strategies of deer procurement and hide production. These expectations facilitate the development of a hunting-for-hides model that provides a backdrop for case study consideration.

Sociopolitical Perspectives on Economic Intensification

Within the domestic economy production activities operate at performance levels well below their potential capacity (Sahlins 1972:41–99). People produce what they perceive they need in order to survive, nothing more, nothing less. Natural resources, labor power, and technological capabilities remain underutilized because the system functions at a level of sufficiency blind to its ability to produce surplus. Economic intensification emerges from the domestic economy to transcend this productive inertia as the interplay of social and political forces embodied in kinship relations (Sahlins 1972:101–148). Intensification, at times, has led to the greater productivity of resources, while under different circumstances it has improved the accessibility or increased the production of resources (Bender 1978:205–206). Its effects on societies have been just as varied, resulting in less labor for equal gains, greater resource yield, or more leisure time. In this study I define intensification as the surplus production of goods, beyond those required by the domestic unit for personal consumption or basic survival needs, that serve social and political purposes that extend outside the immediate household or social group. If the domestic economy can fulfill basic survival needs, why intensify economic activities to produce surplus goods? And, how might this be accomplished?

In many small-scale sedentary societies, economic intensification and the ability to influence surplus production are tightly interwoven with social status and political power. Individuals become leaders by being generous, but to be generous one must first acquire the surplus goods to be given away. Increased productivity often begins within an aspiring leader's own household. Cooperation among several workers increases productivity; therefore, productivity depends to some extent on the size of the domestic unit. An aspiring leader may bring additional workers into the domestic labor force through marriage, adoption, caring for widows, and taking in orphans. By enlarging the domestic work force, a leader can appropriate the labor of more workers whose combined labor output is able to produce surplus goods. Because leaders have the ability to amass more goods than other households, they can give away more goods. The strategic use and distribution of wealth ensures that others remain in their debt—economically and socially. These repeated generous acts accrue the obligations of other households who must reciprocate favors, which enables leaders to accumulate both the goods and people needed to host large community events such as ceremonies, interregional trade, and warfare (Bender 1978:209–214; Collier 1988:72–74; Sahlins 1972:133–136).

A leader's authority and their household's productivity remains limited under these conditions because cultural constraints restrict their ability to control or profit from labor and produce of households other than their own. Furthermore, this type of leadership is temporary because the power of a ruling household dissipates with the senility or death of its founder (Collier 1988:76; Sahlins 1972:138). Under certain circumstances, leaders may extend their authority beyond their own domestic unit and persuade others to contribute their labor toward the greater good of the community. Leaders use their influence to organize communal activities such as large-scale hunts or seasonal harvests whose success requires the cooperative efforts of many households. In this situation, power over labor is always limited because it cannot extend beyond a leader's own household or socially defined kinship bonds for any longer then a brief occasion or ephemeral moment (Arnold 1996:60; Sahlins 1972:139–140).

Along with the ability to appropriate domestic labor and products, the use and exchange of valuables acts as a critical stimulus to the transformation of social and political relations (Arnold 1991; Blanton and Feinman 1984; Lightfoot and Feinman 1982; Peebles and Kus 1977). Whether they are called valuables, wealth items, or prestige goods, these objects tend to be nonlocal or locally scarce items acquired either as raw materials or finished products whose value stems simultaneously from their relative scarcity and high procurement cost (Earle 1987:69). Such items convey multiple cultural meanings, which vary depending on the good, its symbolic value, and the circumstances surrounding its use (Thomas 1991). Prestige goods can mark social status, legitimize political authority, and symbolize associations or distinctions among kin-groups, communities, and regional polities (Hickerson 1996; Scarry 1999; Shennan 1982). They affix a distinctly material component to political relationships because the exchange of valuables can create, maintain, and enhance alliances (Brumfiel 1987:111–112; Earle 1987:71). The use of wealth items to legitimize prestige and power is only effective, however, if other segments of society recognize and desire the goods symbolizing these statuses (Wattenmaker 1998:200).

The perspectives of economic intensification discussed here emphasize that it is the social and political agendas of certain persons or social groups and their efforts to acquire, and perhaps even control, socially valued goods that act as one of the prime motivating factors in the decision to intensify economic activities. Economic intensification, as defined in this study, relates in no way to the risk-management strategy where the accumulation of subsistence items, particularly agricultural produce, serves as a buffer against periods of high stress and low yield. Rather, the significance of intensification is viewed from the perspective of the surplus production of nonsubsistence craft goods for sociopolitical purposes that extend beyond the immediate household or social group. In certain historic Native North American contexts, the motivation to intensify deerskin production and related activities can be directly linked to a desire to participate in a growing trade in hides, furs, and nonlocal goods. The ability to acquire valuables, whether through surplus production or exchange, provides an opportunity to enhance social prestige, increase political authority, and cultivate alliances through the public display, reciprocal giving, and exchange of socially valued objects. In the southern Appalachian Highlands, deerskins may have served a somewhat similar purpose or, rather, as I contend, they may have provided the material resources needed to acquire the nonlocal goods that served these purposes.

In the southernmost Southeast, missionization, rather than trade, defined many of the interactions between Native Americans and Euro-American colonists (Milanich 1994, 1999). Native leaders among the Timucua, Apalachee, and Guale supported the Spanish missions and embraced Catholicism because they believed such actions to be to their advantage. Collaborating with missionaries, and by extension the Spaniards, brought them personal prestige and power, gifts of valued European goods, and alliances with the powerful Spanish colony (Milanich 1999:124). In contrast to Spanish colonial enterprises, interactions between Native Americans and Euro-Americans elsewhere in the Southeast and the Northeast were defined largely, at least initially, by commercial ventures, particularly trade in deerskins and beaver furs (e.g., Braund 1993; Cleland 1993; Heidenreich and Ray 1976; Judd and Ray 1980; J. Martin 1994; Merrell 1989; Rogers 1990; Stine 1990; Usner 1992; R. White 1991). Only one brief, and ultimately unsuccessful, attempt to proselytize local native peoples occurred in the Middle Atlantic region. In 1570 Spanish Jesuits sailed from *La Florida* into the Chesapeake Bay and up the James River to establish a mission at Ajacan. The Jesuits survived less than a year before they were slaughtered by local Algonquians, an event that Seth Mallios (1998) argues was carried out because the missionaries violated the native gift economy.

For these reasons I believe it is appropriate to view trade and exchange as the primary vehicle by which native groups in the southern Appalachian Highlands obtained nonlocal goods. I am not proposing that this trade was limited to commodity exchanges of alienable objects between, as stated by Christopher Gregory (1982:12), reciprocally independent transactors. Gift exchanges, defined by requisite reciprocity and social obligations (cf., Mauss 1925), were common occurrences even after the inception of the deerskin trade, often serving as a prerequisite to other forms of exchange (Braund 1993:30; Merrell 1989:31). Nor am I suggesting that all goods exchanged and received in trade held a static social form. Deerskins and nonlocal goods likely exchanged as commodities in some contexts, but as gifts in others (cf., Gregory 1982). Furthermore, the value of these items within native communities may have depended upon the specific social contexts surrounding their transaction and use (Thomas 1991).

Economic Intensification and the Deerskin Trade

The transition from the production of goods for personal consumption to the production of goods for surplus accumulation requires related-economic activities to be intensified. In the context of the production of deerskins for trade in the southern Appalachian Highlands, this transition would have involved several steps. First, since surplus hides could only be obtained from increased hunting, it would be necessary to alter deer harvest practices in order to ensure that the most effective strategies were employed so that the greatest number of deer could be killed. If acquiring hides for trade was one desired outcome of the hunt, certain factors that influenced the market value of a deerskin might also need to be considered. By increasing the number of deer killed there would be surplus hides available for exchange purposes; however, hide processing must also be intensified in order to properly prepare the deerskins for trade.

Some of the most compelling information on the regional intensity of commercial hide production has survived in eighteenth-century government documents that recorded the annual number of deerskins shipped to Great Britain by the Virginia and Carolina colonies. Between 1699 and 1710, the two colonies combined exported an average of about 68,000 deerskins per year, a total of more than 800,000 hides in little more than a decade (Crane 1928:328). It is apparent from these statistics that Native Americans produced deerskins for trade in astounding quantities by the first decade of the eighteenth century, although these figures likely underrepresent the actual number of hides shipped overseas due to the colonial governments' inability to closely monitor exports. Export numbers, which fluctuated from year to year (Table 1.1), were also influenced by the ever-changing status of relations among and between Native American groups and colonial traders (J. Martin 1994:307–308; Merrell 1989:40–42; Tinling 1977:118) and by colonial laws

Table 1.1. Numbers of Deerskins Exported to Great Britain, 1699–1715.

	Virginia	Carolina
1699–1700	47,578	86,621
1701–2	34,044	100,732
1703–4	35,236	119,352
1705–6	26,351	43,243
1707–8	14,386	153,294
1709–10	36,032	120,446
1711–12	39,157	113,733
1713–14	7,971	111,232
1715	6,843	55,806

Note: Adapted from Crane (1928:328). Year spans from Christmas of the previous year to Christmas of the current year. Information compiled from figures received by the Board of Trade from the Inspector General's Office, Custom House of South Carolina, on June 19, 1716.

that occasionally banned hide export or levied export taxes on hides and furs (Henning 1823a:174, 199, 307, 314, 488, 497; 1823b:185; 1823c:63; Tinling 1977:153).

In return for deerskins, colonial traders supplied Native Americans with a variety of items that grew increasingly diverse over time. In 1612, Captain John Smith reported "copper, beades and such like" to be the primary goods the English traded to local Algonquian peoples in coastal Virginia (Tyler 1907:108). Several decades later, in the early 1670s, John Lederer advised that if one desired to trade for deerskins and other pelts "your best Truck is a sort of course Trading Cloth . . . Axes, Hoes, Knives, Sizars, and all sorts of edg'd tools" as well as guns and ammunition, which were illegal to supply to Native Americans (Lederer 1966:26). It was not long after this that trade merchandise included, "guns, gunlocks, powder, shot, cut flints, small hoes and hatchets, felling axes, scissors, knives, tobacco tongues, beads (great blue and red to the westward, and small black and white to the southward), Jews-harps, tinshears, Redlead, Duffields, Cotton and plains red and blew" along with coffee, sugar, and rum (Ewan and Ewan 1970:385).

Prior to European contact, the interregional exchange of nonperishable prestige goods in the Appalachian Highlands of southwestern Virginia consisted largely of marine shell and copper—materials that Native Americans continued to value as symbols of social status, political power, and religious authority even after the influx of European commodities (Hantman 1990:685; Potter 1989:153; Rountree 1989:71; Waselkov 1989:122). Interactions with Europeans during the early to mid-seventeenth century, the time period that is most relevant to this study, brought the first foreign goods to Native Americans. At this point in time in southwestern Virginia such items were generally limited to copper-alloy ornaments and glass beads, although the same cannot be said about regions closer to colonial settlement. Both archaeological and ethnohistoric evidence suggest that many Native American groups in the greater Middle Atlantic region regarded the earliest glass beads as prestige items along with copper and marine shell (Gleach 1997:57; Hamell 1983:25; Potter 1993:218–219; Rountree 1989:73).

An international demand for deerskins provided a new market for processed hides and new sources of prestige goods that had not previously existed in eastern North America. New sources of socially valued goods, as well as the introduction of new types of goods, can dramatically alter social and political relations both at the village level and on a regional scale (Rogers 1990:17; Sahlins 1985:141–142). Native Americans may have initially sought European objects for their uniqueness or for their similarity to native items that held social and ritual significance (cf., Miller and Hamell 1986). Regardless of precisely why these goods were valued, if surplus deerskins provided the material means to obtain socially valued, nonlocal goods such as marine shell, copper, and glass, certain sociopolitical relationships might also need to be renegotiated to accommodate an expanding access to wealth by persons or social groups who had not previously been in these positions.

Although asymmetrical sociopolitical relationships existed among some late prehistoric societies in the southern Appalachian Highlands, European colonization acted as a critical catalyst in the historic development of these processes. I view European contact as a force that had a significant impact on Native North American cultural systems, but also as a force that some segments of native society, such as certain social groups, entrepreneurial factions, or emergent elites, could have used and manipulated to their own benefit. Increased ambiguity in sociopolitical distinctions can lead to any number of creative responses that serve to reestablish and maintain social differentiations. Under such circumstances, mortuary behavior often becomes a primary medium for competitive displays of status and status aspirations (Cannon 1989; Parker Pearson 1984).

In the following section, I review seventeenth- and eighteenth-century documents regarding colonial markets and modern texts on white-tailed deer bioecology. A knowledge of market standards combined with an understanding of sex-specific deer maturation patterns enables me to develop a model of hunting for the purpose of hide production. Archaeological expectations are then proposed regarding the possible ways this new trade in deerskins may have influenced Native American economic strategies of deer procurement and hide production.

Deerskin Procurement, Production, and Trade

If hide production intensified deer harvest levels would have also increased and this increase in deer exploitation should be evident in seventeenth-century faunal assemblages. Looking for shifts in the age, sex, and seasonality profiles of deer harvests offers one approach for identifying a shift from deer procurement for local consumption to deer hunting for commercial trade. I survey seventeenth- and eighteenth-century written texts to gain a better understanding of the various criteria that may have influenced Native American deer-hunting strategies associated with intensified hide production and trade. What factors affected the market value of a hide? Were large hides more valuable than small hides? Did age or sex of the deer make a difference in the potential worth of the hide? And, was the quality of the hide critical?

John Lawson, an Englishman who traveled throughout the Carolinas in the early eighteenth century, wrote extensively about the natural resources and Native Americans he encountered on his journeys. Deerskins, he contended, were an important commodity of the southern English colonies "provided they be *large*" (Lefler 1967:129, emphasis added). The use of the adjective large may be related to an observation made by other English colonists (Quinn and Quinn 1973:62; Waselkov and Braund 1995:59) and seen in prehistoric and modern white-tailed deer populations today (Purdue 1986); deer that inhabit the piedmont and mountain regions are much larger in size than those found in the flat, coastal plain. If one desired large deerskins, then deer hunted in central and western Virginia would be far preferable to those killed in coastal areas.

Lawson's emphasis on large deer may also be in reference to the sex and age of the animal. In North Carolina, in the early eighteenth century, buckskins held a pound sterling value of about two shillings; doeskins a value of one shilling, six pence; and pricket skins (hides from male deer in their second year) a value of only one shilling (Stine 1990:12). Hides from fawns (male or female deer younger than 12 months of age) were worth about three-quarters of a shilling and registered as the least likely type of deerskin to be purchased by traders (Stine 1990:13). Differences in the relative value of different types of deerskins indicate that hides from adult male deer were worth 25 percent more than hides from adult female deer, 50 percent more than hides from yearling males, and 75 percent more than hides from fawns. Devaluing hides from young deer, specifically young *male* deer, may have been one way the leather industry discouraged Native American hunters from killing deer before they reached a certain age or, from Lawson's perspective, a certain size.

Several other factors also determined the potential worth of a hide. In the late seventeenth century in Pennsylvania, "dressed" buckskins were valued at two shillings, five pence, whereas "undressed" buckskins were worth only one shilling, two pence (Bishop 1864:429). Doeskins brought one shilling, nine pence if "dressed" and only one shilling if "undressed" (Bishop 1864:429). In this instance, hides from male deer were worth up to 30 percent more than hides from female deer, precisely how much more depended on how the hide was processed. This information implies that the value of a deerskin also depended on how completely a hide was processed.

Hide processing involved several labor-intensive steps. To begin, a hide worker washed the skin in water and strung it taut in a sapling frame or stretched it across a log. The skin was then scraped to remove excess flesh and fat and allowed to dry in the sun. Again, it was soaked in water, stretched, and scraped, this time to remove the hair on the outer side. Deer brains mixed with water were worked into the moist hide, which was vigorously twisted and pounded to break down coarse fibers. The hide was again stretched, dried for the final time, and placed over a shallow pit filled with slow-burning wood. This process, known as smoking, colored the hide, the exact hue depended on the type of wood used. Smoking also gave the deerskin a water resistant quality. The final product was a soft, supple, yet very durable, material that exhibited a suedelike finish. Processing time varied from half a day for scraping a skin to well over a week for a fully dressed and smoked hide (Hudson 1976:266–267; Lefler 1967:216; Swanton 1946: 442–448).

Three categories of processed hides were recognized: dressed, half-dressed, and undressed (Braund 1993:88). Dressed skins required the most labor. The hides were cleaned, the hair removed, and they were tanned and smoked. Half-dressed skins, as the name implies, received less preparation. They were scraped to remove flesh and hair and were briefly smoked (Braund 1993:68), probably as an insurance against pest infestation since deerskins were particularly vulnerable to maggots, moths, and other pests (Peake 1954:140–143). William Byrd II whose father had been an authority on trading operations in western Virginia, remarked in the late seventeenth century that deerskins dried over smoke "smell so disagreeably that a Rat must have a good Stomach to gnaw them in that condition" (Bassett 1901:212). Undressed or "raw" skins were minimally processed; the flesh was scraped from the hides to minimize chance of decay, but the hair remained intact (Braund 1993:88). Most deerskins produced for commercial trade were half-dressed by the early eighteenth century (Braund 1993:68; Usner 1992:248). Hide workers had apparently decided that the labor investment required to produce half-dressed hides outweighed the advantages of trading less labor-intensive raw skins that brought a lower exchange rate on the market. By the late eighteenth century, however, production changed to favor raw hides due to pressures from the European leather industry, which disliked native processed skins (Braund 1993:89).

The processed hides acquired through trade eventually made their way to coastal colonial ports where merchants shipped the highest-quality deerskins to England to be manufactured into book covers, fine leather gloves, and other apparel and accessories (Clarkson 1960; Parrish 1972). Traders sold lower-quality or "lighter" dressed hides, those that did not meet market standards, to local leather manufacturers or shipped them to the northern American colonies (Crane 1928:111). In his book *The Southern Frontier,* Verner Crane defines high-quality deerskins as "heavy buckskins, weighing on average close to two pounds when 'half-dressed'" (111). Although Crane chose the word "buckskins" to characterize high-quality deerskins, the term is often used as a colloquial reference to dressed deerskins, regardless of the sex of the animal (Tanners' Council of America 1946:9; International Council of Tanners 1975:14). Crane probably did not intend to specify hides from male deer exclusively, but rather to accentuate the importance of heavier or larger deerskins. By the eighteenth century, traders used both the number of deerskins and pounds of deerskins to calculate hide value or the exchange rate per trade good. While Lawson stressed the importance of large deerskins, those who thought in terms of weight, such as Crane, emphasized heavy skins as bringing the highest market value.

Deerskin weight varied depending on the degree of processing and the size of the hide. Weights ranged from one pound for a dressed doeskin to three or more pounds for a raw hide from a mature buck (Braund 1993:88–89; Waselkov and Braund 1995:245). Hides that weighed too little, less than 15 ounces in some instances, were not considered "merchantable" (McDowell 1955:118). The Carolina Commissioners of Indian Trade passed numerous statutes that established standards and value limits for different types of deer-skins. In 1716, in one of many attempts to regulate intercultural commerce and control profit margins, the commission issued a decree to a Charlestown storekeeper that set the value of dressed skins, weighing a pound or more, at five shillings per pound; dressed light skins at two shillings, six pence or less per skin (the exact rate to be determined by their "goodness"); raw buck skins, weighing one and a half pounds or more, at five shillings per skin; and raw doe skins and all other light skins at two shillings, six pence or less per skin (the exact rate to be determined by their goodness and weight) (McDowell 1955:72).

This survey of historical documents demonstrates that several key components determined the market value of a hide—the weight or size of the deer-skin, the sex of the deer, and the degree of processing. The use of the word "goodness" suggests that other factors may have also influenced how much a hide was worth. In the northeastern fur trade, season of kill governed the quality of a beaver pelt. Beaver fur was at its prime in the winter months, while animals killed during the summer had very little fur and undesirably thick skins (Innis 1962:64–65). Deer hides may exhibit a similar seasonal variation in their coats that would affect the quality of leather. The concept of goodness, however, may also refer to how well the hide was processed, if it had been cleaned thoroughly and scraped evenly, and if it was free of holes, tears, and knife cuts.

In sum, a number of factors, including age, sex, size, degree of processing, and quality, all influenced the potential market value or exchange rate of a deerskin. These factors may be summarized as: (1) large or heavy deerskins held a higher market value than small or light skins, (2) hides from adult male deer were worth more than similarly processed hides from adult female deer, (3) hides from adult deer brought a higher price than hides from young animals, and (4) quality, although not clearly defined, played some role in determining deerskin value. The next question to consider is how this preference pattern may have influenced Native American supply of hides in terms of deer harvest strategies.

White-Tailed Deer Bioecology

The white-tailed deer, *Odocoileus virginianus,* populates diverse edge habitats from coastal marshes to woodlands throughout North and Central America (Halls 1984; Taylor 1956). Taxonomists have identified 30 subspecies of white-tailed deer; the southern Appalachian Highlands supports only *O. v. virginianus* —the true "Virginia" whitetail. This subspecies extends from the Atlantic Coast west to the Mississippi River, and from the northern boundaries of Virginia, West Virginia, and Tennessee, south to southern Georgia, Alabama, and Mississippi (Kellogg 1956:39; Rue 1978:14).

Like most large mammals, white-tailed deer exhibit sexual dimorphism; males are generally larger in both weight and height than females (Severinghaus and Cheatum 1956:76). The most substantial weight gain occurs in white-tailed deer during the first seven months of life, followed by a pause in growth over the winter, and a second significant increase in weight over the next warm season. Males continue to gain weight during their third and fourth years, a trend that is much less apparent in females (Severinghaus and Cheatum 1956:76). A mature buck typically weighs 25 to 30 percent more than a nonpregnant adult doe (Baker 1984:16).

A linear relationship exists between weight and height in white-tailed deer (Severinghaus and Cheatum 1956:75). Bone growth, coinciding with patterns of weight gain, occurs most rapidly between birth and seven months of age followed by a second substantial increase over the next year (Severinghaus and Cheatum 1956:76). Shoulder heights range from 81 to 107 cm, with males slightly taller than females of similar age (Linzey 1998:289; Sauer 1984:81).

Male and female birth ratios can vary slightly. Males tend to be somewhat predominant at birth, although reported statistics differ (Verme and Ullrey 1984:99; Rue 1978:195; Severinghaus and Cheatum 1956:66). Some studies suggest that nutrition levels may influence birth sex ratios. During years of high nutrition, does bear a disproportionate number of female fawns, whereas during times of less than optimal nutrition they produce more male offspring (McCullough 1979:69; Verme 1969). Despite these minor fluctuations, statistics indicate a fairly even distribution of both sexes within a population (Emerson 1980:120; McCabe and McCabe 1997:15).

Modern White-Tailed Deer Populations in Virginia

To better understand the biological relationship between age, sex, and weight in white-tailed deer populations, data were obtained from the Virginia Department of Game and Inland Fisheries on deer killed in the state during the past decade. Law requires deer hunted in Virginia to be registered at one of more than 1,400 big-game check stations. Information on age (based on mandibular tooth eruption and wear), sex, weight, weapon used, and date and county of kill is recorded as part of the Virginia's ongoing deer wildlife management program (Knox 1996:2). I use these data to determine the age

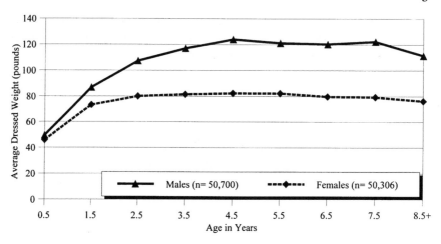

Figure 1.1. Modern white-tailed deer age and weight distribution by sex. Data provided by the Virginia Department of Game and Inland Fisheries.

at which deer within the state reach their peak weight and how these patterns of growth differ between male and female deer.

Based on the average dressed weight of deer killed in Virginia between 1988 and 1998, the most significant weight gain occurs in both sexes between the first and second age classes (.5 to 1.5 years) (Figure 1.1). In female deer, weight gain after 1.5 years of age is minor and no increase is seen beyond 2.5 years of age, at which point a doe has reached her peak dressed weight of approximately 80 pounds (converted live weight is equivalent to 104 pounds following Severinghaus 1949a). In contrast, male deer continue to gain weight between the second and third (1.5 and 2.5 years) and the third and fourth (2.5 to 3.5 years) age classes. It is not until about 3.5 years of age that males attain their maximum dressed weight of about 120 pounds (which reflects a live weight of 154 pounds following Severinghaus 1949a).

These data illustrate that sexual dimorphism is clearly expressed in animals older than 18 months of age. By six months of age, male deer weigh about 7 percent more than female deer, a difference that doubles by 1.5 years of age. In the 2.5-year age class, male deer weigh 25 percent more than female deer. By 3.5 years, a weight difference of about 30 percent exists between male and female deer. This spread gradually increases to 35 percent over the next few years. The significance of these data is not the precise pound weight per age class, because various factors can affect the body weight of deer, but rather the pattern of sex-specific growth.

Insights into sex ratios could also be gained from these data, however biases stemming from state hunting regulations, sex-specific hunting periods, and present-day hunter preference make this information unreliable for inference beyond modern, managed populations.

Hunting for Hides: A Model

An understanding of sex-specific deer maturation coupled with seventeenth-century deerskin preference patterns enables me to develop a model of hunting for the purpose of hide production. This model identifies some of the possible ways Native Americans may have altered deer harvest strategies in order to procure hides that would bring competitive exchange rates. A few additional distinctions must first be made regarding historic categories and value determinants of deerskins.

Differences exist in the market value of a deerskin based on whether the hide was large or small, whether it was heavy or light, and whether it came from a buck, a doe, a pricket, or a fawn. The latter two terms allow important distinctions to be made regarding the meaning of the former groups. The category "pricket," a male deer in its second year of life, emphasizes that this age class is *not* equated with the category "buck." The clear separation between a pricket and a buck is directly related to the sex-specific growth patterns described in the previous section. It is only when a male deer has reached his third year of life (2.5 year age class) that he weighs significantly more than a female deer regardless of age class.

It is also meaningful that a category similar to pricket does not exist for female deer. The absence of such a term coincides with differences between male and female maturation. Female deer attain their adult body weight in their second year of life (1.5 year age class) and little difference exists between the weight of a two-year-old or older doe. The category "fawn," male or female deer younger than 12 months of age, in the absence of a female class equivalent to pricket, reveals that the term "doe" applies to female deer one year of age and older.

Clarifying these distinctions allows me to more clearly define the relationship between different types of deerskins and the sex and age of the deer. A large hide equates with a heavy hide, which equates with a buckskin, which equals a hide from a male deer 2.5 years of age or older. A small hide equates with a light hide, which equates with a doeskin, which equals a hide from a female deer 1.5 years of age or older. Hides from fawns and prickets are most likely lumped under the category "other light skins," while an animal killed too young, one whose hide did not meet market weight standards, would have been deemed unacceptable for trade.

The degree of processing and hide quality also influences the market value of a deerskin. To better understand these relationships I again turn to information gained from white-tailed deer bioecology. Deer go through two molts per year; each time they shed their existing coat and replace it with one more suitable for the upcoming season (Hiller 1996:29; Rue 1962:28, 1978:144–145; Sauer 1984:73–74). During the molting process the roots of the new hairs are visible on the inside of the skin as they grow through the hide. Leather produced from a hide of a deer in molt exhibits a dark appearance and a coarse feel. These are two characteristics considered undesirable, and likely unmarketable, by the leather industry (Schultz 1876:189). In Virginia, the first molt occurs in late spring, generally sometime in May or early June (Stüwe 1986:58). Once deer have shed their insulated winter coats, they wear their summer pelage for three to four months until they begin a second molt in early autumn, sometime in August or early September (Stüwe 1986:60).

Combining this information, if deerskin preference patterns influenced Native American deer harvests, I would expect to see a hunting strategy focused on prime-age deer between 1.5 and 4.5 years of age. I would also expect few animals targeted in the .5 year age class, a greater frequency of adult male deer 2.5 years of age and older, and deer hunted in greatest numbers before and after, but not during, molting season. This model differs from the harvest pattern seen at many Late Woodland sites in southwestern Virginia where hunting strategies generally reflect a pattern of high juvenile kill-off primarily during the fall and winter months with some year-round hunting also evident (Barber n.d.; Barber and Baroody 1977; Barber and Reed 1994; Guilday 1971; McGinnes and Reeves 1957; Waselkov 1977).

Economic Intensification and Cultural Change: Archaeological Expectations

Economic intensification associated with deerskin production for trade should be reflected in the archaeological record of deer procurement and hide processing as well as in the distribution of the nonlocal goods obtained through trade. The degree to which economic activities intensified is likely to vary among households, depending upon individual and family ambition, aspiration, and access to resources, and may occur only within certain households or on a community-wide basis. To determine whether or not economic intensification occurred during the Protohistoric period and how, if observed, this may have effected sociopolitical organization I conduct two key phases of analysis. I first consider general subsistence practices, deer hunting strategies, and deerskin processing activities to measure hide production levels and to begin to gauge who produced hides for trade. The second phase of my research identifies patterns of prestige goods use which, combined with the above analyses, enable me to evaluate evidence for economic intensification and concomitant sociopolitical changes that stemmed from a participation in the deerskin trade. I outline my expectations below, while fully acknowledging that changes in the archaeological records may be more difficult to detect than the expectations suggest. Specific analytical methods used are described along with the data and results in Chapters 3, 4, and 5. My research focuses on information obtained from three Native American village sites located in southwestern Virginia: Crab Orchard (44TZ1), Hoge (44TZ6), and Trigg (44MY3). These sites, along with previous archaeological research in the region, are described in Chapter 2.

Measuring Deerskin Production

Deerskin production is measured from three perspectives: vertebrate fauna subsistence practices, deer-hunting strategies, and deerskin processing activities. General expectations associated with intensified production are described below. If economic intensification associated with deerskin production is not apparent in the archaeological record then it is expected that the variables will remain similar between the Late Woodland and Protohistoric periods.

General Subsistence

I define general vertebrate subsistence practices from a detailed analysis of animal remains to assess the dietary importance of deer and other animals during the Late Woodland and Protohistoric periods. It is expected that the utilization of deer will increase in the Protohistoric period as hide production intensified. In addition to deerskins, the pelts of small fur-bearing animals, particularly beaver, raccoon, and fox, were also processed for trade. The exploitation of these taxa may also increase as the deerskin trade becomes a more important economic activity.

Deer Hunting

If Native Americans hunted deer in part to procure hides for trade, then the market value of deerskins may have influenced choices made by native hunters. I have argued that a number of factors affected the potential market value or exchange rate of deerskins, including age, sex, size, degree of processing, and quality. Based on the hunting-for-hides model developed in the previous section it is expected that as deerskin production intensified Native American

hunters would harvest more prime-age deer, exploit more male than female
deer, and kill deer primarily before and after, but not during, molt. To assess
the validity of these assumptions, I examine three variables: age of deer at
death, sex of deer hunted, and season of deer kill.

Deerskin Processing

I assess deerskin production-related activities in several ways. First, butchery
marks associated with hide removal are isolated to determine if skinning was
performed with the intent of maximizing hide size. Next, I examine the proportions of deer elements present. I then consider the intrasite distribution of
skinning marks and body part frequencies indicative of carcass processing to
delineate activity areas where initial production-related activities may have
occurred. Second, I consider the relative frequencies of tools and features
used to process hides. These data provide another measure of the intensity
of production activities. I also examine the intrasite distribution of hide-
processing tools and features to locate where deerskin production may have
taken place at each site. I expect that as hide production intensified the frequency of skinning marks will increase and hide processing tools and features will become more numerous.

Assessing Prestige Goods Use

To identify sociopolitical changes that resulted from participation in the
deerskin trade, I examine how the valued, nonlocal goods obtained through
interregional trade and gift-exchange were used. Prestige goods can be moni-
tored both by the source of the material and by their cultural context. In
southwestern Virginia most nonlocal goods are found in association with
human remains, therefore my analysis focuses on mortuary assemblages. I
consider the quantity and distribution of nonlocal goods, specifically marine
shell, copper and copper-alloy, and glass, within Late Woodland and Protohistoric burial populations to gain further insights into who was, and who
was not, being buried with these socially valued materials. Funerary rituals,
including the material offerings interred with the dead, provide insights into
social and political relations present in past communities (J. A. Brown 1995;
Hutchinson and Aragon 2002; O'Shea 1996).

During periods when sociopolitical differences are growing increasingly
ambiguous, mortuary behavior often develops into an effective medium for
competitive expressions of social standing that are consciously manipulated
by living social groups (Cannon 1989; Parker Pearson 1984). European contact provided new sources of nonlocal, status-marking goods that had not

previously existed in the southern Appalachian Highlands, while participation in the deerskin trade offered new opportunities to obtain these items. Access to nonlocal goods could have either been restricted or expanded during the Protohistoric period depending on the sociopolitical processes in operation. If the use of nonlocal goods was limited to certain individuals or social groups, I expect that nonlocal artifacts will be restricted in their distribution within the burial population. If all or most persons used these goods, I expect nonlocal artifacts to be more broadly distributed across the burial population.

2 Late Woodland and Protohistoric Archaeology in the Southern Ridge and Valley

Physical Setting

Within the Appalachian Highlands geologic province lies the Ridge and Valley, a region characterized by longitudinal ridges separated by valleys that vary in width. The Ridge and Valley extends for more than 1,450 km from the northern Hudson Valley in New York to central Alabama. In Virginia, this region comprises the portion of the state that lies west of the Blue Ridge Mountains with the exception of a small section of Appalachian Plateau in the southwestern-most corner. The southern half of the Ridge and Valley region in Virginia defines my primary research area (Figure 2.1). The topography here represents some of the most varied in the state. Elevations range from 1,600 to 7,240 km above sea level. Oak and chestnut tree forests are predominant, although mixed mesophytic communities (e.g., basswood, maple, tuliptree, hemlock, beech, and such) commonly grow along ravine slopes (Braun 1964:231–233). Two major watersheds drain the southern Ridge and Valley: the New River, which flows northwest through West Virginia to empty into the Ohio River, and the Tennessee River drainage, comprised of the Powell, Holstein, and Clinch rivers, which flows south into the Tennessee River, then the Ohio River, and eventually the Mississippi River.

Previous Research

Archaeological survey and excavation in the southern Ridge and Valley has provided a wealth of information on Late Woodland (ca. A.D. 1000–1600) and Protohistoric (ca. A.D. 1600–1700) Native American lifeways. Native peoples settled a variety of environmental zones ranging from floodplains to ridges, hilltops, plateaus, and upland valleys (Egloff 1992:211). Hamlets and base camps, from which residents exploited localized, seasonal resources, dotted the landscape. Large semipermanent villages, which tended to be palisaded by the latter part of the Late Woodland period, favored floodplain and upland locales where rich soils supported agricultural activities (M. B. Barber

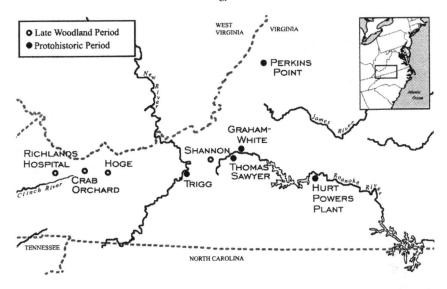

Figure 2.1. Location of the archaeological sites in southwestern Virginia mentioned in the text.

1989a:20; Egloff 1987:48, 1992:212). Upland environments north of the study region have been shown to provide high-potential soils for maize horticulture and, compared to valley floors, a shorter frost-free-day growing season (W. Johnson and Athens 1998). Native subsistence strategies combined cultivating crop plants with hunting terrestrial animals and harvesting wild nuts and fleshy fruits. Fishing and other aquatic resource exploitation supplemented the diet. Vertebrate fauna resource utilization focused on white-tailed deer with substantial dietary contributions from black bear and wapiti. Wild turkey and box turtle were also procured in significant numbers (M. B. Barber n.d., 1989a; Barfield and Barber 1992). Other taxa such as squirrel, raccoon, passenger pigeon, quail, and various fish, especially catfish, provided diet diversity (M. B. Barber 1989b, 1999; Barber and Baroody 1977; Moore and Lapham 1997; Whyte 1999). Wild plant foods consisted of hickory, black walnut, various weedy plants, and grape, to name a few. Domesticated crops included corn, beans, and possibly squash (Benthall 1969:143; Egloff and Reed 1980:146; Geier 1983:251, 262; Gremillion 1993a; L. Johnson 1982:41).

The importance of maize horticulture to Native American subsistence in the southern Ridge and Valley is debatable (e.g., see Barfield and Barber 1992). Bioarchaeological research on collagen stable isotopes extracted from human remains that included 44 individuals from four sites in southwestern Virginia has suggested that most Ridge and Valley peoples ate a diet rich in maize, possibly 50 to 90 percent of all plants consumed (Trimble 1996:77–80). Because other studies have cautioned that past diet is most accurately assessed by examining stable isotope samples from both collagen and apatite carbonate (Ambrose and Norr 1993; Norr 1995, 2002; Ubelaker and Owsley 2003), the validity of this conclusion is uncertain. While the bioarchaeological data potentially indicate that maize comprised a major dietary staple in Ridge and Valley subsistence, the ethnobotanical data paint a very different picture. Maize and other cultigens are recovered infrequently compared to wild plant remains at Late Woodland and Protohistoric sites located along the Jackson River in the Gathright Dam area (Geier 1983:269; Geier and Warren 1982:147; Whyte and Geier 1982:114). These data suggest that maize may have been less important in some areas of the Ridge and Valley than in others. A similar pattern of regional variation in maize use, which has been attributed to differences in local ecology and sociopolitical circumstances, is also evident elsewhere in the Southeast (Hutchinson et al. 1998; Larsen et al. 2001).

European domestic plants have not been identified in southern Ridge and Valley archaeobotanical assemblages; however, elsewhere in the greater Southeast imported species such as peach, watermelon, and cowpea are found on sites dated as early as the late seventeenth century (Gremillion 1987, 1993a, 1993b). The European domestics that southeastern Native Americans incorporated into their subsistence practices share three common characteristics: they were dietary supplements, not staple foods; the plants thrived in local environments; and they had high yield relative to labor investment (Gremillion 1993b). Some low-ranked indigenous plant resources declined in use as Native American peoples devoted more time and labor to trade-related activities, such as deer hunting and hide production, during the late seventeenth and early eighteenth centuries (Gremillion 1987:276). Overall, however, historic native plant use saw only minor shifts in the proportions of indigenous species that contributed to the diet following the incorporation of European domestic plants (Gremillion 1987:277).

The effects of European colonization on vertebrate fauna subsistence are not yet fully understood for the southern Ridge and Valley, although in surrounding areas Native American animal utilization practices display considerable continuity between the late prehistoric and historic periods (M. B. Barber, M. F. Barber, and Bowen 1996; Holm 1987; Pavao-Zuckerman 2000; Reitz 1991). Animal remains from the Graham-White site (44RN21), a mid- to late-seventeenth-century settlement located along the Roanoke River, show a greater reliance on white-tailed deer and a decline in the diversity of non-fur-bearing animals, changes that likely resulted from participation in the deerskin trade (Moore and Lapham 1997). Only one specimen from an animal species introduced by Europeans has been recovered to date in a seventeenth-century context in southern Virginia. Archaeologists found the maxillary canine of a domestic male pig from deep within a sealed pit feature at the early-seventeenth-century Hurt Powers Plant site (44PY144), a settlement located along the Roanoke River in the western Piedmont roughly 64 to 80 km downstream from the Graham-White site (M. B. Barber, M. F. Barber, and Bowen 1996:284). How the tusk arrived at the village is uncertain, as is its use and meaning to the site residents. By the late seventeenth and eighteenth centuries, European-introduced animals such as cow and horse had entered some southeastern Native American economies, but these domesticates remained marginal in their importance to native diet for many decades (Pavao-Zuckerman 2000).

Changes in seventeenth-century economic activities also brought about changes in how these activities were performed. In the southern Ridge and Valley and adjacent regions, for example, a bone tool called a beamer was used to scrape hair and fatty debris from deerskins during the initial processing stage. Beamers first appear on archaeological sites within the Roanoke River drainage in the western Virginia Piedmont ca. A.D. 1250, although small numbers are occasionally found in earlier contexts on sites in the northern North Carolina interior (M. B. Barber 2003:171). With the inception of the deerskin trade during the early to mid-seventeenth century, the production and use of beamers increased throughout the region (Barber 2003:174–177; M. B. Barber, M. F. Barber, and Barfield 1997). Bone tool distributions from the southern Ridge and Valley support this observation. The late Late Woodland Shannon site (44MY8), a large palisaded village dated ca. A.D. 1550–1600, yields more than 35 bone tool artifacts including awls, chisels, projectile points, and fishhooks, but not a single beamer (Benthall 1969:78–89). In contrast, at the Protohistoric Perkins Point site (44BA3) beamers comprise five out of seven bone tools with all beamers showing extensive use wear (Whyte and Geier 1982:14). Bone beamers as well as stone tools declined in use during the late seventeenth century, at least in northern North Carolina, since edged metal tools could be obtained in more regular supply through direct trade with Europeans (Holm 1987:253; Ward and Davis 1993:449).

During the Late Woodland and Protohistoric periods, Native American mortuary practices display a preference for flexed interments in the southern Ridge and Valley (MacCord 1989a:100–101), although burial treatments also include single primary (extended and flexed), multiple primary, and secondary (bundle) burials as well as interment in caves and, possibly, stone cairns and ossuaries (Boyd and Boyd 1992:256–258; Boyd et al. 2001; Egloff 1987:46). Mortuary behavior differs from the northern Ridge and Valley and western Piedmont where accretional burial mounds dotted contemporaneous landscapes (Dunham 1994; Dunham, Gold, and Hantman 2003; Gold 1999;

Hantman 1990, 2001; MacCord 1986). Several earthen mounds have also been recorded along the Holstein and Clinch Rivers in four southwestern Virginia counties (Egloff 1987; Holland 1970). These mounds, located within the Tennessee River drainage, are associated with Mississippian-era chiefdoms rather than Eastern Woodland polities (Egloff 1987; for a summary of Mississippian cultural traits in southwestern Virginia see Jefferies 2001).

Burial features in the southern Ridge and Valley vary in form from simple pits to central chamber and to shaft and chamber pits. Interments are found throughout the village, in central locales as well as peripheral areas adjacent to the palisade and outside as well as inside domestic structures. Grave offerings generally occur in one-third to one-half of the burials at a site (Boyd and Boyd 1992:256; MacCord 1989a:101). Nonperishable grave goods include marine shell, bone beads and pendants, bone and stone tools, ceramic vessels, smoking pipes, the occasional copper object, and, during the Protohistoric period, copper-alloy ornaments and glass beads. The general mortuary complex in the southern Ridge and Valley suggests the presence of high-status persons, although concrete evidence for ranking and ascribed status is lacking (Boyd and Boyd 1992:256; Egloff 1992:214).

The interregional exchange of nonperishable prestige goods, which consisted mainly of marine shell and copper prior to European colonization, increased during the Late Woodland period throughout the southern Middle Atlantic region (Stewart 1989, 1995). These status-marking goods moved through well-defined, broad-based exchange networks, although in the southern Ridge and Valley the abundance of buscycon, marginella, and olivella shell ornaments suggests that these objects were hoarded by individuals in some communities (Stewart 1989:64). Distribution patterns for copper artifacts, which are found in much lower frequencies than marine shell, suggest either focused exchange or hoarding. In general, few sites in the southern Ridge and Valley yield copper. At the Shannon site (44MY8), a copper object of undetermined form was recovered from the grave of an older adult male (Benthall 1969:93) and an effigy-like copper pendant and a rolled cone tinkler were found in a burial at the Richlands Hospital site (44TZ51) (Egloff and Turner 1988:19). Spectrographic analysis determined that the copper from both sites had been mined from a North American source (Egloff and Turner 1988:19), however elsewhere in eastern North America the tinkler ornament form has been associated exclusively with historic contexts (e.g., Bradley 1977:11; Kent 1984:203–204; Kraft 1972:52; Mayer-Oakes 1955:122; M. Smith 1987:37; Wall and Lapham 2003:166–167; Wells 2002:99). Copper and copper-alloy artifacts have also been recovered from two of the three study sites, Crab Orchard (44TZ1) and Trigg (44MY3). These items will be discussed in detail in Chapter 5.

Salt from the present-day Saltville area in Smyth County was another valued trade item during the Late Woodland period (M. B. Barber and Barfield 2000). By the early seventeenth century, European trade brought glass beads, copper-alloy, and the occasional iron artifact to some southern Ridge and Valley communities (Barber 1989a; M. B. Barber, M. F. Barber, and Bowen 1996; Geier and McFee 1981; Geier and Warren 1982; MacCord 1977; Whyte and Geier 1982). Edged iron tools and guns entered the region by the mid- to late seventeenth century as evidenced by the find of a trigger from an English-manufactured snaphaunce firearm at the ca. A.D. 1660–1680 Graham-White site (44RN21) (Klatka and Klein 1998). Both copper and marine shell continued to be valued by Native Americans, however, even after the introduction of European commodities. For example, in northeastern Virginia, the early historic grave of a high-status person, possibly a petty chief, contained local and nonlocal goods, including five shell mask gorgets engraved with stylized human faces, plain shell gorgets, tubular shell beads, and several complete whelk shells, along with numerous copper-alloy items, glass beads, and a metal cross (Potter 1993:213).

In the Middle Atlantic region, copper, in particular, gained importance in prestige exchange relations late in the Late Woodland period, beginning around ca. A.D. 1400 (Hantman 2001). Leaders among the Algonquian-speaking Powhatan peoples considered copper to be a key symbol of political power and religious authority (Hantman 1990:685; Potter 1989:153). The importance placed upon this metal by the Powhatans in the early seventeenth century led English colonists to comment on the great value bestowed upon this metal by coastal Algonquian societies (Rountree 1989:86). Although copper obtained considerable symbolic significance in most Eastern Woodland societies (Hantman 1993:109), some argue that it never reached the social importance in the Late Woodland period in southwestern Virginia as it did elsewhere to the north and east (M. B. Barber, Solberg, and Barfield 1996:17).

The social significance and meaning conferred upon European-manufactured glass beads is slightly more ambiguous than that of copper and marine shell. Substantial archaeological and ethnohistoric evidence suggests that many Native American groups in the greater Middle Atlantic region identified the earliest glass beads as prestige items (Gleach 1997:57; Hamell 1983:25; Potter 1993:218: Rountree 1989:73). Glass beads have been found in association with high-status burials (Potter 1993:218–219) and ritual paraphernalia (Hamell 1983:24, 27). Virginia trader William Byrd I complained in the late seventeenth century that a "want of beads" often resulted in unsuccessful exchanges if his trade goods stock did not contain the specific types and colors of glass beads requested by his Native American trading partners (Tinling 1977:14, 64).

Late Woodland sociopolitical organization in the Middle Atlantic region has

most recently been characterized as precariously balanced between egalitarian-
ism and hierarchy (Hantman and Gold 2002). If and when the emergence of
elite individuals and limited ranked social systems occurred, they were infrequent events confined to particular geographic locales. Elite power, which relied on the control of some status-defining activity such as ritual behavior or
interregional trade in prestige goods, was plagued by instability. Other members of society eventually challenged elite control causing power to either
shift or collapse. Martin Gallivan (2003) has argued that after A.D. 1200
social inequality became institutionalized in some parts of the Middle Atlantic, which led to the development of powerful, yet unstable, chiefdom polities.

One or more chiefdoms emerged for a brief time in the southern Ridge
and Valley (Barber and Barfield 2000; Custer 1986; Egloff 1987, 1992; Gardner 1979; Meyers 2002; Turner 1983). One simple chiefdom developed along
the Holston River drainage in Smyth and Washington counties sometime
after A.D. 1350. Specialists in the Saltville Valley mined salt deposits and
produced salt for trade. Local leaders, who controlled the trade, exported salt
to southeastern Mississippian societies in exchange for prestige goods such
as marine shell gorgets, mica, and copper (M. B. Barber and Barfield 2000).
It has also been speculated that two other chiefdoms, aligned more closely
with the Mississippian frontier, formed in Lee County and Scott County, the
two southwestern-most counties in Virginia (Meyers 2002). These proposed
chiefdoms are situated south of the study region, so while these data are suggestive, additional research is needed to determine the nature of political
systems and the degree of social inequality that existed elsewhere in the
southern Ridge and Valley region.

Previous archaeological research provides important information on Late
Woodland Native American lifeways and some insights into Protohistoric societies in the southern Ridge and Valley. There is much that remains unknown about similarities and differences in Native American lifeways between these two periods, however. In the following section I describe the
three study sites that provide the comparative data I use to gain a better
understanding of cultural change and continuity between Late Woodland
and Protohistoric native communities.

The Study Sites

My research focuses on three Native American village sites: Crab Orchard
(44TZ1), Hoge (44TZ6), and Trigg (44MY3). These sites are located within
an 80 km radius of one another in the southern Ridge and Valley region in
southwestern Virginia (see Figure 2.1). Two of the villages, Crab Orchard and

Hoge, were occupied late in the Late Woodland period, ca. A.D. 1450–1600. The third village, Trigg, was occupied during the Protohistoric period ca. A.D. 1620s to 1650s. Data from the Late Woodland villages provide a baseline for assessing change and continuity in economic organization and sociopolitical systems at the Protohistoric settlement.

The Crab Orchard Site

The Crab Orchard site (44TZ1) is located along the Clinch River in the Pisgah Valley about 6 km west of the town of Tazewell. Robert D. Wainright first documented the site in 1914, following which he notified the Smithsonian Institution that he had found an "old Indian town" while visiting Tazewell County (Wainright 1914 in MacCord and Buchanan 1980:3). In 1947, Smithsonian Institution archaeologist Joseph Caldwell traveled to the Crab Orchard site to investigate local reports of human remains discovered in a nearby rockshelter. During his visit to the site, Caldwell acquired a small assemblage of ceramic sherds collected by the landowner, Jeffrey Higginbotham. A brief description of the pottery was published in the *Archeological Society of Virginia Quarterly Bulletin* (Caldwell 1951). In 1963, C. G. Holland returned to the Crab Orchard site as part of the Smithsonian Institution's archaeological survey of southwestern Virginia, a project funded by the National Science Foundation (Holland 1970:40). He dug a test trench on the site that produced a small collection of ceramic and lithic artifacts, of which most dated to the Late Woodland period (Holland 1970:40).

Large-scale archaeological investigations at the Crab Orchard site began in the early 1970s when a road relocation by the Virginia Department of Transportation threatened to destroy part of the village. In 1971, the Virginia State Library in conjunction with the Archeological Society of Virginia undertook salvage excavations in the area of the site located within the construction right-of-way (MacCord and Buchanan 1980:5). These excavations, directed by Howard MacCord, Sr., targeted a narrow strip of land that ran through the center of the village and areas along the north and south edges of the site (Figure 2.2). Excavations continued sporadically for the next four years. Approximately 50 percent of the village was unearthed, a total area of about one acre. Artifact recovery methods during these 1971–74 excavations relied primarily on handpicking, as excavators collected only the artifacts visible to them while shoveling or troweling (MacCord and Buchanan 1980:110).

In 1978, the Virginia Research Center for Archaeology returned to the Crab Orchard site to conduct further excavations following notification from Tazewell County that another portion of the site could be disturbed by the proposed construction of a social services building (Egloff and Reed 1980:

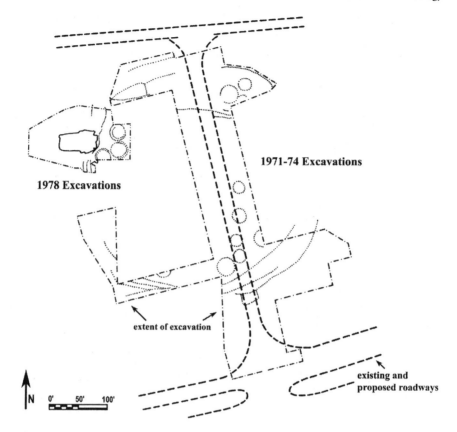

Figure 2.2. Plan map of the Crab Orchard site. Adapted from MacCord and Buchanan 1980:Figure 3.

131). Excavations focused on an area in the northwest portion of the village. Field recovery techniques included sifting feature fill through 6 mm mesh hardware. In addition, archaeologists water-screened soil samples from select proveniences through 6 mm standard and fine mesh hardware to recover microflora and microfauna (Egloff and Reed 1980:132).

The most recent excavations to date took place in 1985 when Calvert McIlhany, under contract by Tazewell County officials, conducted further testing in the general area of the village. He excavated two additional portions of the semisubterranean structure first identified during the 1978 investigations (McIlhany 1986).

Radiocarbon dates for the Crab Orchard site suggest that the village was occupied late in the Late Woodland period, sometime during the sixteenth century (Table 2.1). One ^{14}C sample taken from a burial feature (Burial

Table 2.1. Radiocarbon Dates from the Crab Orchard, Hoge, and Trigg Sites.

Site	Sample	Conventional Date	Reference
Crab Orchard	Beta 15426	A.D. 1420 ± 60	McIlhany 1986
(44TZ1)	UGa 479	A.D. 1570 ± 120	MacCord and Buchanan 1980
	UGa 2816	A.D. 1610 ± 55	Egloff and Reed 1980
	UGa 2912	A.D. 1805 ± 60	Egloff 1992
	UGa 2815	A.D. 1870 ± 60	Egloff and Reed 1980
Hoge	Beta 119056	A.D. 1340 ± 60	Jones and MacCord 2001
(44TZ6)	Beta 119057	A.D. 1500 ± 80	Jones and MacCord 2001
	Beta 119058	A.D. 1640 ± 60	Jones and MacCord 2001
	UGa 2453	A.D. 1660 ± 170	MacCord and Buchanan 1980
Trigg	UGa 4490	A.D. 1575 ± 60	Buchanan 1984
(44MY3)	Beta 178705	A.D. 1630 ± 60	Klatka 2003, pers. comm.
	Beta 178706	A.D. 1630 ± 30	Klatka 2003, pers. comm.
	UGa 4489	A.D. 1715 ± 80	Buchanan 1984

9) yielded a date of A.D. 1570 ± 120 (MacCord and Buchanan 1980:150). Charred timbers from within the semisubterranean structure produced a date of A.D. 1610 ± 55 (Egloff and Reed 1980:132). A third sample from the bottom of a storage pit (Feature 511A) returned a date much too late in time to be considered accurate (A.D. 1870 ± 60) (Egloff and Reed 1980:136). A fourth sample, taken from charred timbers found on the floor of the semisubterranean structure, returned a date of A.D. 1420 ± 60, which, when compared to previous dates, appears too early to be accurate (McIlhany 1986:38).

Features

The 1971–74 excavations uncovered 12 domestic structures, 74 storage pits, 168 burials, 14 hearths, three possible smoking pits, and several other miscellaneous features (MacCord and Buchanan 1980:11, 78, 109). Multiple palisade lines surround one to two concentric rings of circular-shaped domestic structures that are organized around a central plaza (MacCord and Buchanan 1980:108). The stockade walls measure approximately 125 m in diameter, an area that encloses about three acres. These dimensions make the Crab Orchard site the largest palisaded Native American village recorded in Virginia to date (MacCord and Buchanan 1980:5).

The 1978 excavations yielded an additional three domestic structures, evidence of three palisade lines, numerous storage pits, 17 burials, several hearths, and a rectangular-shaped, semisubterranean structure (Figure 2.3) (Egloff and Reed 1980). This semisubterranean structure is unique in southwestern Virginia. It measures 19.5 m east to west, 9 m north to south at the western edge, and flares to 12 m at its eastern end (Egloff and Reed 1980:132). The building overlaps two palisade lines while a third stockade circumvents the eastern wall. The placement of internal features denotes two to three building periods. Internal features include large support posts, interior wall posts, a central hearth, and a bench that runs along the northern interior wall (see Egloff and Reed 1980:Figure 5). The western half of the bench appears as a .3 m wide ledge that broadens to a 1.5 to 2 m wide bench in the eastern part of the building. The original floor surface extends 23 cm below subsoil. Its unusual size, architecture, and internal features suggest that this structure served a special purpose such as a community meeting house for various secular and religious activities. Structures similar in size and shape have been found along the Powell and Clinch rivers in eastern Tennessee and at the Fort Ancient Buffalo site (46PU31) in West Virginia (Egloff and Reed 1980:147).

Ceramics

Ceramic artifacts from the 1971–74 field seasons total more than 17,850 pottery sherds (MacCord and Buchanan 1980:119). Limestone-tempered Radford series ceramics are predominant (83 percent) (Figure 2.4 and Table 2.2). Radford series pottery is restricted in distribution to southwestern Virginia, particularly the New and Tennessee River drainages, between A.D. 1000–1700 (Egloff 1987:11). More than 70 percent of the Radford sherds show either cord-marked or plain surface treatment. Net-impressed and corncob-impressed ceramics are also present in low frequencies. Several limestone-tempered sherds that exhibit a complicated-stamped surface treatment have been tentatively identified as stylistically similar to PeeDee or Lamar ceramics (MacCord and Buchanan 1980:119–120; Figure 2.5). Both Peedee and Lamar cultures are associated with Mississippian societies that occupied regions south of the Pisgah Valley (Coe 1995; Williams and Shapiro 1990). Shell-tempered New River ceramics are present at 16 percent of the 1971–74 ceramic assemblage (MacCord and Buchanan 1980:119). About one-half of the sherds exhibit gastropod shell temper and one-half display mussel shell temper (MacCord and Buchanan 1980:121). Sand-tempered ceramics account for only 1 percent of the collection (MacCord and Buchanan 1980:122).

The 1978 excavations, which concentrated on the northwest portion of the Crab Orchard village, recovered an additional 1,931 ceramic sherds (Egloff and Reed 1980:139). Again, limestone-tempered Radford wares (85 percent)

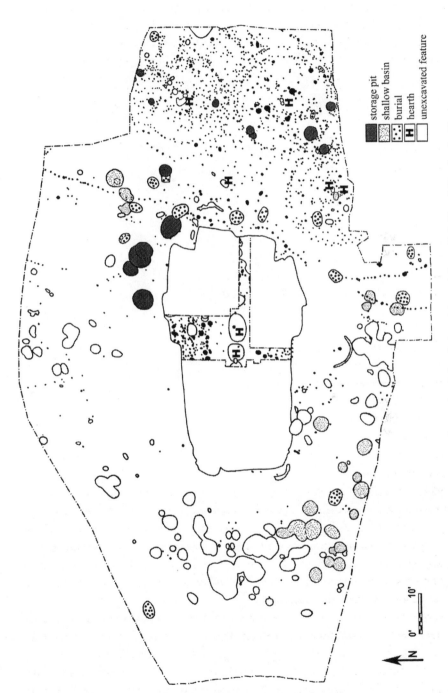

storage pit
shallow basin
burial
H hearth
unexcavated feature

N

0'   10'

Figure 2.3. Plan map of the 1978 excavations at the Crab Orchard site. Adapted from Egloff and Reed 1980:Figure 2.

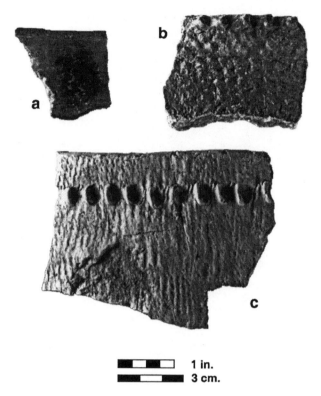

1 in.
3 cm.

Figure 2.4. Limestone-tempered ceramic sherds from the Crab Orchard site,
(a) plain, (b) net-impressed, (c) cord-marked. Image provided by Keith Egloff,
Virginia Department of Historic Resources.

are most common. Cord-marked surface treatment comprises 43 percent of
these ceramics. Corncob-impressed limestone-tempered sherds are also present in small numbers. Shell-tempered sherds account for 13 percent of the
1978 ceramic assemblage (see Figure 2.6). More than 80 percent of the shell-
tempered ceramics exhibit a plain or smoothed-over surface treatment that is
characteristic of late Mississippian-influenced cultures in eastern Tennessee.
In addition, two complicated-stamped sherds tempered with crushed quartz
are present (Egloff and Reed 1980:139). The design appears to be characteristic of Qualla wares, a late prehistoric to historic period ceramic associated
with the Cherokee peoples in western North Carolina (Egloff 1987:35).

Fauna and Flora

Both periods of excavation produced large assemblages of animal remains
(Egloff and Reed 1980:141; MacCord and Buchanan 1980:110–111); unfortunately, marked differences in the recovery techniques that were implemented

1 In.

3 cm.

Figure 2.5. Limestone-tempered, complicated-stamped ceramic sherds from the Crab Orchard site. Image provided by Keith Egloff, Virginia Department of Historic Resources.

during excavation have resulted in highly disparate collections. During the 1971–74 investigations, excavators most often handpicked feature fill, very occasionally dry-screened fill, and never floated fill (MacCord and Buchanan 1980:110). Prior to beginning my research I conducted a visual survey of the faunal materials recovered from this period of fieldwork. My examination revealed that excavators only occasionally saved animal remains and almost never deer bone. If and when excavators did save fauna they chose fairly complete specimens easily identifiable to animal species less common than deer such as bear, wapiti, or dog. It is well known that handpicking severely biases species representation as well as the skeletal elements recovered (Payne 1972, 1975). Samples biased by lack of sieving also compromise quantitative comparisons with faunal assemblages recovered by screening methods (Shaffer 1992). Due to these biases I elected not to analyze the faunal material from the 1971–74 excavations.

In contrast to earlier fieldwork, the archaeologists participating in the 1978

Figure 2.6. Mussel shell–tempered ceramic sherds from the Crab Orchard site, (a–b) plain with incised decoration, (c) plain, (d) smoothed-over cord-marked. Image provided by Keith Egloff, Virginia Department of Historic Resources.

excavations at the Crab Orchard site used 6 mm mesh hardware to sift soil and water-screened select soil samples through both standard and fine mesh hardware specifically to ensure the recovery of tiny plant remains and animal bones (Egloff and Reed 1980:132). The faunal assemblage from these latter excavations is described and interpreted in the following chapters.

The recovery methods employed during the 1971–74 field seasons undoubtedly biased the botanical assemblage as well, although both wild and domesticate plant remains were identified from feature contexts (Egloff and Reed 1980:111). Wild plant remains along with cultivated domesticates, including corn and possibly beans and squash, were recovered during the 1978 investigations (Egloff and Reed 1980:146). A detailed analysis of these botanical materials has not yet been completed (Keith Egloff, personal communication).

Table 2.2. Comparison of the Ceramic Assemblages by Temper Type.

	Limestone Temper	Shell Temper	Sand Temper
Crab Orchard, 1971–74 Excavations	83% (*n* = 14,872)	16% (*n* = 2,810)	1% (*n* = 141)
Crab Orchard, 1978 Excavations	85% (*n* = 1,640)	13% (*n* = 253)	—
Hoge	97% (*n* = 54,841)	1% (*n* = 656)	1% (*n* = 654)
Trigg	41% (*n* = 21,611)	10% (*n* = 5,036)	47% (*n* = 24,675)

Note: The 1–2 percent of ceramic sherds not accounted for in this table are tempered with either crushed quartz, sand, grit, or steatite. Sources of data: MacCord and Buchanan (1980:Tables X–XII), Egloff and Reed (1980:Table 1), Jones and MacCord (2001:Table VII), and Buchanan (1984:327–328).

The Hoge Site

The Hoge site (44TZ6), located about 16 km east of the Crab Orchard site, lies near Burkes Garden Creek in the town of Burkes Garden in Tazewell County. Its history is similar to that of the Crab Orchard site. Robert D. Wainwright first reported the location of the village to the Bureau of American Ethnology, Smithsonian Institution, in 1914 (Jones n.d.). Almost 50 years later, C. G. Holland recorded the site as part of the Smithsonian Institution's archaeological survey of southwestern Virginia, but he was unable to pinpoint its exact location at that time (Holland 1970:40). Emory Eugene Jones, a member of the Archeological Society of Virginia, became intrigued by the mystery of the "lost" Hoge site and visited Burkes Garden in 1971 in an attempt to relocate the village. Four years of searching led to its rediscovery on the Hoge family property in northeast Burkes Garden.

In 1976, Jones began initial testing of the site. Howard MacCord, Sr., acted in an advisory capacity on the project, consulting with Jones on site excavation and interpretation (Jones n.d.). Excavations continued on an intermittent basis for almost 20 years, during which time Jones uncovered about 40 percent of the village. Recovery strategy included dry sifting soils through 6 mm mesh hardware (Jones and MacCord 2001:115). Unlike most archaeological sites in the region, the buried features here had not been

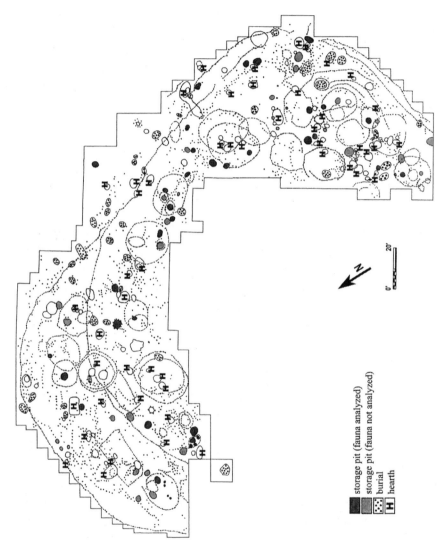

Figure 2.7. Plan map of the Hoge site. Adapted from Jones and MacCord 2001:Figure 22.

storage pit (fauna analyzed)
storage pit (fauna not analyzed)
burial
H hearth

N

0'   20'

harmed by agricultural activities. Jones passed away in 1996 after several years of declining health. Since then, MacCord has tackled the enormous task of compiling Jones's field notes and observations, conducting analysis on thousands of artifacts, and writing the final site report that was published in 2001 as Special Publication Number 40 by the Archeological Society of Virginia.

Four carbon samples were submitted for standard dating, one in 1978 and three others more recently in 1998 (see Table 2.1). The dates returned as A.D. 1340 ± 60 years (Feature 114), A.D. 1500 ± 80 years (Feature 11), A.D. 1640 ± 60 years (Feature 82), and A.D. 1660 ± 170 years (Feature 19) (Jones and MacCord 2001:176–177; MacCord and Buchanan 1980:150). They suggest a late fifteenth- to sixteenth-century occupation for the Hoge village.

Features

The Hoge village exhibits a layout similar to the Crab Orchard site with a palisade surrounding numerous domestic structures that encircle a central plaza (see Figure 2.7). Two well-defined palisades are evident with at least three additional paralleling or adjoining lines of postholes noted. The outermost palisade, which measure 72 m by 61 m, enclose an area slightly less than one acre (Jones and MacCord 2001:117). Features include 22 presumed domestic structures, 19 smaller structures possibly used for storage, 75 storage pits, 37 burials, and more than 60 hearth areas. In addition, a rectangular structure that measures 6.7 m by 3.7 m was uncovered in the northern section of the village. Its precise function is unclear (Jones and MacCord 2001:121).

Ceramics

Ceramic artifacts total more than 56,000 pottery sherds. Limestone-tempered Radford wares comprise 97 percent of the assemblage, 87 percent of these sherds exhibit net-impressed surface treatment (Jones and MacCord 2001: 140–142) (see Table 2.2). Other wares identified include sand-tempered Wythe ceramics (1 percent), a regional variant of Dan River ware, and shell-tempered New River ware (1 percent). Of the shell-tempered New River sherds, one-third exhibit gastropod temper and two-thirds display mussel temper. Gastropod temper is most common late in the Late Woodland period, but declines in popularity with the introduction of mussel-tempered pottery (Egloff 1987:12).

Fauna and Flora

Approximately 7,300 animal remains were recovered from feature fill and more than 17,000 specimens from midden areas (Jones and MacCord 2001:

173–174). A detailed analysis of the fauna recovered from feature contexts is presented in the following chapters. The botanical collection is small, but contains both wild and domestic plants including acorn, hickory nut, plum, corn, and bean (Jones and MacCord 2001:175–176).

The Trigg Site

The Trigg site (44MY3), located approximately 72 km east of the Hoge site and 89 km east of the Crab Orchard site, is situated on the southeast bank of the New River within the present-day city limits of Radford. Historic land use includes farming, industrial activities associated with the nearby Norfolk and Western Railroad, and a late-nineteenth-century planing mill that once stood just outside the southeast boundary of the site (Buchanan 1984:1). Similar to the Crab Orchard and Hoge site histories, C. G. Holland (1970:20) recorded and surveyed the Trigg site during his 1963–64 archaeological survey of southwestern Virginia, a project conducted in collaboration with the Smithsonian Institution and funded by the National Science Foundation. In the early 1970s, the Radford city government announced its plans to build a recreational park on the land, the construction of which would destroy the site (Buchanan 1984:4). The Virginia State Library in conjunction with the Archeological Society of Virginia and the City of Radford began intensive salvage excavations at the Trigg site in 1974 and returned for a second field season in 1975. Howard MacCord, Sr., directed the project, William Buchanan assisted. Field recovery techniques included sifting feature fill through 12 mm mesh hardware. Soil samples from select features were wet-screened specifically to collect archaeobotanical remains (Buchanan 1984:317). A grant from the Virginia General Assembly through the Virginia Historic Landmarks Commission funded artifact analysis and report writing (Buchanan 1984:4).

There has been much debate about when Native Americans occupied the Trigg village, so much so that the Roanoke Regional Preservation Office, Virginia Department of Historic Resources, recently ran two new ^{14}C dates (Thomas Klatka 2003, personal communication). The two original radiocarbon dates differed significantly (see Table 2.1). One carbon sample from a storage pit (Feature 416) produced a date of A.D. 1575 ± 60. Another sample from a refuse-filled pit feature with 17 postholes encircling its edge (Feature 110) yielded a much later date, A.D. 1715 ± 80 (Buchanan 1984:415). Clifford Boyd (1993:4) has estimated based on the most recent dendrocalibration figures that these two dates compute to A.D. 1490 with a minimum to maximum one sigma range of A.D. 1440–1640 and A.D. 1660 with a probable one sigma date range of A.D. 1620–1810. Unlike the first two dates that were run sometime in the 1970s or early 1980s, the more recent dates are

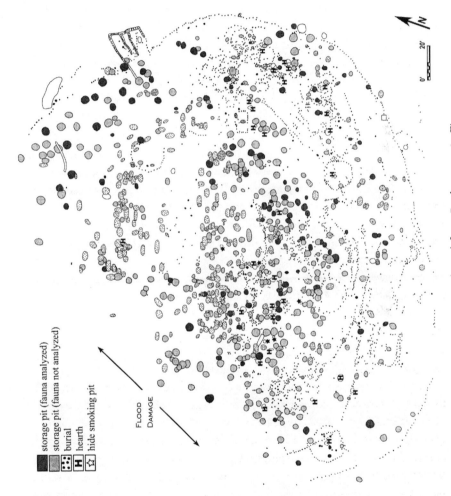

storage pit (fauna analyzed)
storage pit (fauna not analyzed)
burial
hearth
hide smoking pit

FLOOD
DAMAGE

N

0'   20'

Figure 2.8. Plan map of the Trigg site. Adapted from Buchanan 1984:Figure 3.

very consistent with one another. A standard radiometric analysis of bone collagen from Feature 84 returned a date of A.D. 1630 ± 60 (A.D. 1440–1670 calibrated). An AMS analysis of maize from Feature 640 returned a date of A.D. 1630 ± 30 (A.D. 1480–1650 calibrated) (Thomas Klatka 2003, personal communication).

The occupation debate is not limited solely to radiocarbon evidence. Mac-Cord (1977:67) has suggested based on the glass bead artifacts that the Trigg site dates to the first quarter of the seventeenth century. Information gleaned from the artifact assemblages, together with radiocarbon dates, led Buchanan (1984:415) to estimate that the village was occupied ca. A.D. 1600–1635, a date range similar to that proposed by MacCord. Patricia Sternheimer (1983:51), who draws on local lithic and ceramic sequences as well as Mac-Cord's glass bead analysis and a historic reference to the village, has argued that the site was inhabited from the sixteenth through the middle seventeenth century. An even later date has been proposed by Boyd (1993:5) who suggests that the site was occupied ca. A.D. 1630–1670 based on more recent glass bead studies and a reconsideration of the radiocarbon dates. Based on my own analysis, I believe the glass beads to be most characteristic of a ca. A.D. 1620s to 1650s assemblage. This information, combined with the most recent radiocarbon dates run by the Virginia Department of Historic Resources in 2003, leads me to estimate that the occupants of the Trigg site began acquiring European goods in some quantity during the 1620s and continued to participate in regional trade until the site was abandoned sometime prior to or during the early 1650s.

Features

The Trigg village contains 10–29 domestic structures that encircle a small central plaza area (Buchanan 1984:316; Sternheimer 1983:23). Excavations detected two to three palisade walls, the largest of which enclosed about 2¾ acres (Buchanan 1984:316; MacCord 1984:178). Approximately 762 features remained intact despite extensive flooding in the northwest section of the village (see Figure 2.8). Flooding destroyed an estimated 15–20 percent of the site (Buchanan 1984:4). Features identified include 422 storage pits, 278 burials, 40 hearths, five smoking pits, numerous postholes, and several other miscellaneous features (Buchanan 1984:5).

Features, primarily burials, and midden contexts contain European-manufactured goods (Buchanan 1984:322–323). These artifacts provide evidence that the Trigg village residents had access to European trade goods, probably via long distance exchange networks that linked Ridge and Valley groups to Native American communities in coastal areas. Numerous marine shell ornaments found at all three study sites indicate that these exchange spheres had been active long before Europeans arrived in the Americas.

Ceramics

The Trigg site yields more than 52,000 ceramic sherds from feature contexts (see Table 2.2). Sand-tempered Wythe ceramics comprise slightly less than one-half (47 percent) of the assemblage (Buchanan 1984:327–328). Wythe ceramics are limited in distribution to sites located west of the Blue Ridge Mountains, although this pottery is considered to be a regional variant of Dan River wares that are found in southern Virginia and the northern North Carolina interior (Egloff 1987:12). Dan River ceramics are associated with Late Woodland Siouan-speaking groups inhabiting the Roanoke and Dan River drainages ca. A.D. 1300–1700 (M. B. Barber, M. F. Barber, and Bowen 1996; Davis 1987; Egloff 1992; Ward and Davis 1993). Wythe ceramics may postdate A.D. 1500 in the study region, especially when net-impressed and plain exteriors are the predominate surface treatments (Egloff 1987:12). At the Trigg site, most (67 percent) of the sand-tempered Wythe ceramics exhibit net-impressed surface treatment (Table 2.2).

Limestone-tempered Radford series pottery comprises 41 percent of the ceramic assemblage with net-impressed sherds most common (83 percent). Figure 2.9 pictures a limestone-tempered, plain vessel with applied decorative nods and paddle-edge decoration along the rim and incised decoration on the shoulder and body. This vessel was recovered from a storage pit (Feature 451) (M. Klein, Martin, and Duncan 2003). Shell-tempered sherds, which are consistent with New River wares, comprise 10 percent of the assemblage. Net-impressed (48 percent) and plain (33 percent) surface treatments are predominant (Buchanan 1984:328). Figure 2.10 pictures a shell-tempered vessel with corncob-impressions applied over knotted-net impressions. This vessel was also recovered from a storage pit (Feature 110). In addition, two quartz-tempered, complicated-stamped sherds were recently identified from a large storage pit (Feature 640) (M. Klein, Martin, and Duncan 2003).

Fauna and Flora

A basic identification of animal remains from 69 out of 693 cataloged lots identified 24 species including 17 mammals, two birds, four reptiles, and one amphibian (Buchanan 1984:317). Deer and box turtle were most prevalent followed by catfish, turkey, wapiti, bear, squirrel, beaver, and raccoon. Little additional information was gained from this preliminary faunal analysis beyond a list of the identified taxa and their relative rank within the sample. Another study, conducted by Jerry McDonald (1984), focused on identifying

3 in.

8 cm.

Figure 2.9. Limestone-tempered, plain ceramic vessel with incised decoration from a storage pit (Feature 541) at the Trigg site. Image provided by Keith Egloff, Virginia Department of Historic Resources.

harvest profiles of white-tailed deer based on aged mandibles. MacDonald determined that hunters at the Trigg site most often killed adult deer, although he detected no distinct hunting season. He concluded that hunters selected adult animals because they would have yielded a high return of biomass (McDonald 1984:466). McDonald makes no mention of the importance of obtaining large hides for trade purposes. I present a detailed analysis and interpretation of the animal remains from 111 storage pit features from the Trigg site in the following chapters.

The Trigg site excavations also recovered wild and domestic plant remains. Plant species include acorn, hickory nut, hazelnut, walnut, pumpkin, corn, bean, and squash (Buchanan 1984:318). A stable isotope study conducted by Carmen Trimble (1996), which sampled bone collagen from 17 human buri-

3 in.
8 cm.

Figure 2.10. Shell-tempered, net-impressed ceramic vessel from a storage pit (Feature 110) at the Trigg site. Image provided by Keith Egloff, Virginia Department of Historic Resources.

als, determined that maize comprised at least half, if not more, of all plants consumed by the Trigg site occupants. This study relied solely on bone collagen data, which has been shown to be a more reliable measure of diet when it is considered in conjunction with stable isotopes from bone apatite carbonate (Ambrose and Norr 1993; Norr 1995, 2002; Ubelaker and Owsley 2003).

Site Summary and Comparison

Both similarities and differences are apparent in the architecture and material culture seen at each study site. General settlement patterns are nearly identical among the sites in terms of the presence and number of palisades, the organization of domestic structures and associated features, and the presence of a centrally located plaza. Based on site plan and feature data, the Crab Orchard site has been interpreted as a village that was inhabited continually throughout a number of building periods, rather than as a settlement occupied at several disparate points in time (Egloff and Reed 1980:132; MacCord and Buchanan 1980:108). Similarities in village layout between the Crab Orchard, Hoge, and Trigg sites suggest that the same prolonged habitation applies to the latter two villages as well.

Differences exist among the sites in village size as well as in the total area excavated (Table 2.3). The Hoge site, at approximately one acre in area, is significantly smaller than both the Crab Orchard (3 acres) and Trigg (2¾ acres) sites. The percent of the total site area excavated is also less at the Hoge site (40 percent) than at either the Crab Orchard (50–60 percent) or Trigg (80–85 percent) sites. Site density figures indicate that the largest village, Crab Orchard, has the lowest overall number of structures and features per acre. Hoge contains a higher density of both structures and features than Crab Orchard, but a lower number of human burials than either of the other two sites. Feature density is greatest at the Trigg village, with the exception of the number of structures identified by posthole patterns. The low number of domestic structures identified at the Trigg site is likely due to the nature of the excavations, which were salvage efforts, and the rapid pace at which the excavations occurred.

The three ceramic assemblages exhibit differences in the preferred tempering agent as well as surface treatment. The Hoge site pottery is the most homogenous in appearance, being represented almost exclusively by limestone-tempered Radford wares. In contrast, the Trigg site ceramics exhibit the greatest diversity of pottery types, including sand-tempered Wythe wares, limestone-tempered Radford wares, and shell-tempered ceramics. Cultural influences seem to have come from various directions. Relationships with Siouan-speaking Dan River groups to the south and southeast are particularly evident. Interactions with Fort Ancient and Monongahela peoples to the north are also apparent in the material culture from the Trigg site (MacCord 1984:179). The Crab Orchard assemblage, with its high frequency of mussel shell–tempered ceramics and plain surface treatment, shows the greatest evidence of interaction with Mississippian cultures in eastern Tennessee and other areas of the Southeast.

Outside cultural influences are strongly linked to the geographic location of the site and its associated river system. The Clinch River, along which the Crab Orchard site is located, flows south-westward from its headwaters just north of Tazewell into Watts Bar Lake in east-central Tennessee where it then

Table 2.3. Summary Statistics for the Crab Orchard, Hoge, and Trigg Sites.

	Crab Orchard (44TZ1)	Hoge (44TZ6)	Trigg (44MY3)
Total Site Acreage	3	1	2 ¾
Percent Excavated	50–60%	40%	80–85%
Excavated Acreage	1½–1¾	ca. ½	ca. 2¼
No. of Palisades	3	2 +	2–3
Palisade Dimensions	125 m dia.	60–72 m dia.	90 m plus dia.
No. of House Structures	15	22	10–29
No. of Hearth Features*	± 21	60	40
No. of Storage/Refuse Pits	± 89	75	422
No. of Burials	185	38	278
Pit to Burial Ratio	1:2	2:1	1:1.5
No. of Hide Smoking Pits	3 possible	0	5
Miscellaneous Features	1 semisubterranean structure, numerous shallow basin features	19 storage structures, small rectangular structure	

*Note: The Hoge site hearth count includes numerous burned areas that may or may not be formal hearths.

connects to the Tennessee River, the home to various Mississippian populations. The location of the Crab Orchard village in a fertile upland valley, about 770 m above sea level, near several major prehistoric trail networks likely placed the village in an ideal position to control access through the nearby mountain gaps (Egloff 1992:212). The Trigg site, at an elevation of 530 m above sea level, lies along the New River, which originates in western North Carolina, flows north-westward through Virginia, meets with the Galley River in south-central West Virginia to form the Kanawha River that then connects to the Ohio River near Point Pleasant, a town on the West Virginia–Ohio border. Fort Ancient and Monongahela peoples made their homes in the lower and upper Ohio River Valley, respectively. The Hoge site, which shows the lowest diversity and the least evidence of interregional interaction, lies in a remote upland valley 960 m above sea level. The village is located near Burkes Garden Creek, a tributary of Wolf Creek, which flows north and eventually meets the New River at Narrows, a town located near the Virginia–West Virginia border. Burkes Garden is the highest valley in Virginia with surrounding mountain ridges that rise to about 1,340 m in some areas.

While the three study sites are by no means exact replicas of one another, many common attributes are apparent. Keith Egloff (1992:204) has argued that these similarities reflect the regionalization of peoples who shared common cultural and linguistic bonds. The linguistic identity of the site occupants has been hypothesized based on ceramic data. Although one-to-one associations between a specific pottery ware and language is problematic, some general observations can be made. Sand-tempered Dan River and Wythe wares have been historically documented as occurring at sites associated with Siouan-speaking groups (Egloff 1992:203). Limestone-tempered Radford and shell-tempered New River series ceramics may also represent Siouan-speaking peoples (Egloff 1992:203). Settlement patterns at all three study sites are also characteristic of contemporary Siouan groups that occupied areas to the east and southeast rather than Mississippian and Cherokee peoples who inhabited lands to the south and southwest (cf., Jefferies 2001; Petherick 1987; Polhemus 1987; Schroedl 1986; Schroedl, Boyd, and Davis 1990; Ward and Davis 1993). Considered together, the Crab Orchard, Hoge, and Trigg sites provide a unique opportunity to examine Native American societies during the crucial period of cultural change, immediately prior to and following European colonization.

3 Ridge and Valley Animal Exploitation

To assess the dietary importance of deer and other animals during the Late Woodland and Protohistoric periods I define general vertebrate subsistence practices from a detailed analysis of faunal assemblages from the Crab Orchard, Hoge, and Trigg sites. More than 32,800 animal remains were analyzed to achieve this goal. Because of the sizable sample as well as the large amount of data collected I divide my discussion of the vertebrate fauna into two chapters. In this chapter, I outline the basic methods used in my analyses and evaluate how the taphonomic history of each assemblage may affect interpretation of the animal remains. I then examine the general composition of the three assemblages and discuss the specific taxa present in each. In the following chapter, Chapter 4, I examine three specific aspects of deer procurement and use: hunting strategies, butchery practices, and hide processing.

Basic Analytical Methodology

The faunal assemblages were analyzed using modern comparative skeletal collections and published reference sources housed in the Archaeobiology Program Laboratory, National Museum of Natural History (NMNH), Smithsonian Institution. I also utilized collections from the Department of Vertebrate Zoology in identification. The NMNH holds one of the largest and most historically important collections of vertebrate specimens in the world.

The data collected on each faunal specimen differed based on the level of identification that I could achieve for that particular specimen. For specimens that I could identify to the taxonomic level of order or lower, the data recorded included taxon, skeletal element, element side and portion, degree of epiphyseal fusion, evidence of human, animal, and natural modifications, and bone weight (to .1 g). Possible modifications ranged from specimens that were burned, butchered, worked, gnawed, digested, weathered, or root-etched to those that showed use wear, exhibited a pathology, and such. Additional information was collected on modified specimens, the specifics depended upon the modification. For burned specimens, for example, I noted degree of burning and percent burned. Butchered specimens had detailed information recorded about the location, orientation, and type of butchery mark. The methods used to analyze butchered deer bone and antler are described in Chapter 4. I identified only a few miscellaneous worked specimens that had been overlooked when the worked bone artifacts were first separated from the general vertebrate fauna prior to my analysis of the collections. These specimens represent a fraction of the total worked sample so they will not be discussed here.

Taxonomic classification and common name adhere to standards recommended by the Integrated Taxonomic Information System (ITIS) (http://www.itis.usda.gov). Most zooarchaeological studies diverge from ITIS on the species name for domestic dog. *Canis familiaris* has been the favored binomial nomenclature in zooarchaeological literature (Morey 1986, 1994; Olsen 1985; Reitz and Wing 1999:281–282; see also Gentry, Clutton-Brock, and Graves 2004). ITIS considers *C. familiaris* to be a junior synonym and therefore an invalid species name for domestic or feral dog, even though it has page priority in *Systema Naturae* over its wild progenitor, *C. lupus*, gray wolf (Linnaeus 1758). Don Wilson and DeeAnn Reeder (1993:281), the editors of *Mammal Species of the World*, make this change in the publication's second edition where *C. familiaris* is listed as a synonym for *C. lupus* (see also http://www.nmnh.si.edu/msw). Other researchers argue that because *C. familiaris* has been accepted and used worldwide for more than 200 years it should continue to be used for the domestic derivative (Gentry, Clutton-Brock, and Graves 1996, 2004). To remain consistent with ITIS I use *C. lupus* as the species name for both gray wolf and domestic dog. Common name differentiates between the two animals.

Specimens that could not be identified to the taxonomic level of order or lower were sorted by class (i.e., mammal, bird, fish, and such) and then by size (i.e., large mammal, medium mammal, and such). The following size categories apply to these specimens: very large mammal (wapiti), large mammal (deer and bear), medium mammal (dog, fox, raccoon), small mammal (rabbit and squirrel), large bird (turkey, goose, eagle), medium bird (grouse, hawk, and such), and small bird (quail, woodcock, and such). All additional information that could be ascertained from these specimens was also collected (such as skeletal element, element side, fusion, modifications, and such). Bones that could not be assigned to class were counted, weighted, and degree of burning noted.

The taxa present in each faunal assemblage are summarized in Table 3.5. In this table I order the taxa by class and then by taxon body weight, from heaviest to lightest. This is the most appropriate method for data presentation because I use this information to examine the dietary contributions of each taxon. Capture quantities being equal, larger animals have the body mass potential to contribute more to the diet than do smaller animals. For the correct phylogenetic ordering of these taxa, consult the American Ornithologists' Union (1998), Collins and Taggart (2002), Frank and Ramus (1995), McKenna and Bell (1997), Nelson (1994), Sibley and Monroe (1990), and Wilson and Reeder (1993).

Four measures are used to describe the basic composition of the faunal assemblages: (1) bone count, also known as the number of identified specimens (NISP), (2) bone weight in grams, (3) minimum number of individuals (MNI), and (4) biomass. Advantages and disadvantages of each measure are discussed below. Additional analyses appropriate to my research goals were performed on white-tailed deer specimens. These include a detailed study of butchery marks and skeletal element distributions, collecting metric measurements, and assessing age, sex, and season of death. The methods used and data results for some of these analyses are described in Chapter 4.

NISP and MNI

Both NISP and MNI are common measures used by zooarchaeologists to estimate relative frequencies of taxa. Because there has been extensive discussion on the definition of these two terms and their strengths and weaknesses (e.g., Casteel 1977; Grayson 1978, 1979; R. Klein and Cruz-Uribe 1984:24–26; Lyman 1994a; Reitz and Wing 1999:191–202; Ringrose 1993), my summary here will be brief.

NISP is the number of identified specimens per taxon regardless of whether the specimen can be identified to class, family, or a lower taxonomic level. MNI, in contrast, is the smallest number of individuals necessary to account for all identified bones within a single taxonomic unit. Generally, MNI is calculated only for specimens identified to species. Like all measures that archaeologists use to interpret their data, NISP and MNI have their faults. Both measures are affected by past cultural practices, site formation processes, and field and laboratory procedures. NISP is also sensitive to bone fragmentation. It can overrepresent animals with a greater number of skeletal elements or more identifiable elements. In addition, NISP overemphasizes the importance of animals brought back to the occupation site intact versus those butchered in the field. In comparison, MNI is less sensitive to degree of bone fragmentation and is affected less by variations in the number of skeletal elements because of the way the measure is calculated. MNI is affected by sample size, however, in that it overrepresents less common species or species with fewer identified elements. It also varies depending on how one decides to aggregate the data. For example, MNI for a site-wide sample will be less than MNI for each provenience tallied separately. In this study, I calculate MNI on a site-wide basis from paired elements with age of identified taxon taken into account.

Although NISP and MNI measure taxonomic abundance, neither provides a good estimate of the relative contribution of different taxon to the diet (Bowen 1996:92; Grayson 1984:22–23). To obtain this information, I use a measurement known as biomass.

Biomass

The concept of biomass stems from zoological research on allometric growth (Schmidt-Nielsen 1984). When two dimensions of an organism grow in such a way that the growth ratio between the two dimensions remains relatively constant over time, allometric growth has occurred. This scaling relationship is found among animals that vary greatly in size as long as the species considered belong to the same taxonomic class. Biomass estimates are based on the principle that a predictable exponential relationship exists between the size of the parts of an animal and the size of the animal as a whole (Reitz and Wing 1999:68).

To calculate biomass, a mathematical relationship between two body-part dimensions (one part and one whole) must first be established (Reitz and Wing 1999:67–71). Part may be defined as the length or width of a skeletal element or the weight of a specimen. Whole can be the length, width, or weight of an animal. Establishing this relationship is accomplished by plotting some predefined part, such as skeletal weight, on the X-axis of a scatter diagram against a whole, such as total animal weight, on the Y-axis. A regression line is then fitted to these variables by the method of least squares. The regression method examines changes in one variable relative to the other. If the linear relationship between these variables proves to be a good fit statistically then it can be used to predict the value of Y (the whole) for a given value of X (the part).

Allometric scaling works with the same fundamental principal, but it uses a logarithmic rather than linear scale. Logarithmic scales are more useful when comparing relative changes as opposed to absolute changes. The mathematical formula that describes the allometric growth curve and allows biomass to be calculated is $Y = aX^b$ where a is the Y-intercept and b is the slope. In this study, the dependent value Y, the archaeological unknown, is the total weight of an animal and independent value X is the weight in grams of the archaeological specimen. The values of allometric constants a and b are derived from studies by Reitz and colleagues where allometric regression was used to describe the relationship between skeletal weight and total weight

(Reitz and Cordier 1983:Table 2; Reitz and Wing 1999:Table 3.4). Biomass, defined in this study as an "estimate of the total weight that the archaeological specimen weight may represent" (Reitz and Wing 1999:227), is calculated from the total specimen weight per taxon for all taxa except commensals (i.e., mice, rats) and amphibians, the latter of which has no associated regression formula.

Biomass, like NISP and MNI, has both strengths and weaknesses. Biomass provides a better estimate of the relative contribution of different taxon to the diet than many other approaches, such as meat weights, because the method is based on a proven biological relationship (Reitz and Wing 1999:227). In addition, relationships of allometric growth exist for all living organisms, from the prehistoric past through the present day. This eliminates biases found in some zooarchaeological measures that predict the relative dietary significance of a taxon based on the estimated ratio of specimen weight to the average meat weight of a modern animal (see discussion of the weight method by Casteel 1978). Furthermore, biomass maximizes the use of faunal data because, unlike MNI, it can be calculated for all taxonomic units (Reitz et al. 1987:314). In terms of disadvantages, biomass is affected by sample size and how one chooses to aggregate the data (e.g., by specimen, feature, or on site-wide basis) (Jackson 1989). Using specimen weight to predict biomass also carries with it all the biases that initially influence this variable such as preservation, leaching, and mineralization (Reitz and Cordier 1983:247; Wing and Brown 1979:126).

General Assemblage Composition

During 1998 and 1999, a combined total of more than 32,800 animal remains were analyzed from the Crab Orchard, Hoge, and Trigg sites. I identified at least 49 different species, including 23 mammals, 15 birds, two fishes, six reptiles, and three amphibians. A Graduate Fellowship from the Virginia Museum of Natural History supported the initial study of faunal remains from several features at the Hoge site. My main analysis was funded by an in-residence Predoctoral Fellowship at the National Museum of Natural History, Smithsonian Institution. The animal remains, and general artifact collections, are currently curated at the Virginia Department of Historic Resources in Richmond.

The Site Samples

The Crab Orchard faunal sample contains more than 15,700 animal remains recovered during the 1978 excavations from 24 features and a midden area.

The features include 12 storage pits, 10 shallow basin or clay borrow pits, and two hearths. Six of the storage pits are located within domestic structures and six are located northeast of the semisubterranean structure (see Figure 2.3). The two hearths and midden area are located at the center of this structure. Two of the shallow basin features are located within domestic structures, six are located near the palisade (three to the north and three to the south of the semisubterranean structure), one is located west of the central hearths within the semisubterranean structure, and one is located in the cluster of shallow basin pits in the southwest corner of the excavations. Prior to my analysis of the animal remains, David Clark and students enrolled in his zooarchaeology course at Catholic University in Washington, D.C., conducted a preliminary study of the materials from a few select proveniences. This analysis, begun in 1980, was never completed. The materials were later returned to the Virginia Department of Historic Resources following which, in 1998, I borrowed the collection for my research.

As discussed in the previous chapter, the archaeologists who excavated the Crab Orchard site in 1978 sifted feature fill through 6 mm mesh hardware and water-screened soil samples from select proveniences through standard and fine mesh hardware to ensure the recovery of microflora and microfauna. Field recovery methods at the Hoge and Trigg sites included dry-screening only. To make the three faunal assemblages more comparable to one another I choose to exclude the wet-screened materials from the Crab Orchard site in my current analysis. The wet-screened materials comprise 20 percent of the total faunal assemblage (but only 5 percent of total weight), 50 percent of the specimens are unidentified and 44 percent are identified only to class. In addition, 92 percent of the wet-screened materials come from a single storage pit (Feature 511A) at the Crab Orchard site. Specimen weight averages .32 g per specimen, a mean far below that of the dry-screened materials (1.6 g). Only one species present in the wet-screened materials was absent in the dry-screened sample, pied-billed grebe (*Podilymbus podiceps*). I made the decision to exclude these materials in my current analysis after a close examination of the dry- and wet-screened data, which revealed that little new information had been gained from the wet-screened materials. I therefore concluded that little information would be lost in their exclusion here. The faunal sample from dry-screened contexts, which will be described in detail in this chapter, consists of 12,540 specimens from the 24 features and midden area described in the previous paragraph.

The Hoge faunal assemblage contains more than 5,550 animal remains from 51 features. Features include 34 storage pits, four features identified as hearths, seven burials, three areas associated with storage structures, one area associated with a domestic structure, and two features of unknown function. The seven burial features included in this study contained large amounts of midden refuse in the general fill that was not associated with the human remains. All features are well distributed throughout the site, with the exception of the four so-called hearths that cluster in the southeast section of the village (see Figure 2.7).

The sampling strategy I employed for the Crab Orchard and Hoge assemblages includes an analysis of animal remains from all storage pits that contained fauna. Animal remains from the shallow basin features at the Crab Orchard site were also studied. Additional features were selected for analysis based on the quantity of faunal remains recovered, with larger sample sizes (> 30 specimens) being preferable for inclusion.

The Trigg faunal sample contains more than 11,500 animal remains from a sample of 111 storage pits. These features are well distributed throughout all areas of the village (see Figure 2.8). The 111-feature sample includes all storage pits in which the fauna had retained its provenience following a postexcavation fire at the storage facility that initially housed the artifacts. This fire burned a large portion of the artifact assemblage and destroyed many provenience labels. Local archaeologists along with a group of dedicated volunteers from the Archeological Society of Virginia spent many hours carefully sorting through the debris to correlate bags of artifacts with provenience tags in order to minimize the damage that had been done by the fire. Their hard work paid off and a significant proportion of the collection was salvaged. To determine which bags of animal remains had retained their original provenience following the fire I compared prefire specimen counts from Buchanan's 1984 site report to postfire specimen counts from the Virginia Department of Historic Resources data inventory records. This systematic survey revealed that faunal remains from 111 storage pits, out of 422 total storage features, had retained their provenience within a 10 percent margin of error. The 111-feature sample constitutes 26 percent of the total number of storage pits. The sample of animal remains that I then analyzed comprises an estimated 22 percent of the total fauna recovered from the site.

It has been advised to use caution when combining data from different types of features for analytical purposes, especially when zooarchaeological or archaeobotanical data are used to investigate intrasite activities and seasonal patterns (Dickens 1985). This is a valid concern for all archaeological research; however, I believe that it is appropriate to group together the fauna from different feature types for this study. Prior to making this decision I conducted an intrasite examination of the basic composition of the faunal samples from each feature type. At the Crab Orchard site, animal remains from storage pits comprise 85 percent of NISP (almost 90 percent of total weight), while the shallow basin pits and proveniences located within the semisubterranean structure (two hearths, one shallow basin pit, and a midden area) comprise about 7 percent each. The faunal assemblages from these three contexts are similar in regard to the animal species present. White-tailed deer, black bear, wapiti, and box turtle comprise 96–98 percent of NISP of the specimens identified to the taxonomic level of order and lower. At the Hoge site, animal remains from storage pits and burial features comprise 76 percent of NISP. These two types of features are most similar in terms of the type and proportion of species present. Deer, black bear, wapiti, and wild turkey comprise 95 percent of NISP of the specimens identified to the taxonomic level of order and lower from storage pits and burials, while these four species total 99–100 percent of the identified specimens from the areas associated with the storage and domestic structures, hearths, and the features of unknown function. At both the Crab Orchard and Hoge sites, the total number of animal species identified increases as sample size increases. While a detailed examination of the fauna on a feature-by-feature basis may reveal differences in assemblage composition among the various feature types, this initial comparison suggests that strong intrasite similarities exist in the taxa present and the frequency at which they occur.

Table 3.1 presents some basic summary figures for the three faunal assemblages. Data include the number of features with fauna analyzed, NISP, weight, MNI, biomass, average weight per specimen, total species identified, the number of species per taxonomic class, and field recovery techniques.

Taphonomic Biases

The preservation and spatial distribution of animal remains is altered by the interactions of multiple taphonomic agents and processes, both prior to and following burial (Behrensmeyer 1991; Gifford 1981; Lyman 1987a, 1994b). Human activities that have an impact on animal remains range from selective hunting and carcass transport to food processing, meat redistribution, consumption, and refuse disposal, to name a few. Scavenging by domestic dogs also furthers bone dispersal, modification, and destruction. In addition, differential preservation conditions contribute to the survival or attrition of faunal materials, as do archaeological field recovery methods, laboratory processing techniques, and analytical procedures. In this section I compare several attributes of the faunal assemblages to identify how taphonomic biases might potentially affect intersite and intrasite interpretations regarding general as-

Table 3.1. Summary of the Faunal Assemblages.

	Crab Orchard	Hoge	Trigg
No. of Features Analyzed	24	51	111
NISP	12,540	5,564	11,525
Weight (g)	19,736.8	32,066.8	49,811.5
MNI	81	79	264
Biomass (kg)	204.8	333.4	437.4
Average Weight per Specimen (g)	1.6	5.8	4.3
Total Species Identified	27	24	43
No. of Species per Class			
Mammals	15	14	22
Birds	8	5	11
Fishes	—	—	2
Reptiles	2	5	6
Amphibians	2	—	2
Recovery Techniques of Analyzed Fauna	dry screen– 6 mm mesh	dry screen– 6 mm mesh	dry screen– 12 mm mesh

semblage composition. Further discussion of destructive processes affecting deer specimens is presented in Chapter 4.

The faunal assemblages from all three sites exhibit good to excellent preservation, with the Crab Orchard collection falling on the lower end of this scale. I rarely noted physical erosion or root damage. Weathering, which can indicate prolonged exposure to an open-air environment (Behrensmeyer

1978), is absent. Observed surface modifications include carnivore and rodent gnawing and digested, burned, and butchered specimens. Carnivore gnawed bone, which in a village context most often signifies the presence of domestic dogs, is present in all three assemblages. These specimens account for about one-half of 1 percent of NISP at the Crab Orchard site (Table 3.2). The Hoge and Trigg settlements exhibit higher frequencies of chewed bone (3.7 percent and 3.1 percent of NISP, respectively). Domestic canid is also represented at the Crab Orchard site by four dog burials (Features 94, 104, 260A, 260B) (MacCord and Buchanan 1980). In addition, the Trigg site contains isolated dog bones in five features (Features 58, 197, 205, 283, and 400). All three assemblages also contain small numbers of digested and rodent gnawed bone.

Butchered specimens, identified by cut and hack marks, are present in similar proportions at the Hoge (1.0 percent NISP) and Trigg (1.3 percent NISP) sites (Table 3.2). The Crab Orchard assemblage contains a much lower frequency of butchered bone (.2 percent NISP), a pattern that holds even when all unidentified fragments are excluded from the equation. White-tailed deer specimens comprise the majority of butchered bone at the Crab Orchard (91 percent NISP) and Trigg (93 percent NISP) sites, while they are less common at the Hoge site (83 percent NISP). Butchery of deer will be discussed in greater detail in the following chapter. Black bear radius and bacculum account for the remaining butchered bones at the Crab Orchard site. At the Hoge site, butchery marks are found on wapiti pelvis and astragalus, black bear rib and radius, gray fox mandible, and large mammal rib and long bone. The Trigg assemblage shows butchery on black bear humerus, femur, and fourth metatarsal, mountain lion tibia, gray fox mandible, large mammal rib and long bone, and large bird long bone.

The proportion of burned bone varies within each assemblage. Burned bone is categorized as burnt (burned brown), carbonized (burned black), or calcined (burned gray/white). Burned specimens occur most frequently in the Crab Orchard assemblage where more than two-thirds (38 percent NISP) of the fauna exhibit some degree of burning (Table 3.2). Interestingly, storage pits contain 32 percent of the burned bone, while hearth features account for only 5 percent of the burned sample. Within each respective sample, however, burning occurs much more frequently on specimens from hearth contexts. Burning is present on 38 percent of all storage pit fauna and 74 percent of specimens from hearth contexts. Burned specimens comprise 5 percent of NISP of the Hoge collection and less than 2 percent of the Trigg assemblage. Only 3 percent of specimens from hearth contexts at the Hoge site are burned. This frequency is lower than fauna found in storage pits and burials at the Hoge site where burning accounts for 5 percent and 8 percent, respec-

Table 3.2. Summary of Bone Modifications.

Taxonomic Level	Crab Orchard		Hoge		Trigg	
	% NISP (n = 12,540)	% Weight (19,736.8 g)	% NISP (n = 5,564)	% Weight (32,066.8 g)	% NISP (n = 11,525)	% Weight (49,811.5 g)
Carnivore Gnawed	.8	4.6	3.7	10.5	3.1	9.0
Rodent Gnawed	*	*	.1	*	.1	.2
Digested	.1	.1	.2	*	.3	.1
Butchered	.2	1.5	1.0	3.5	1.3	5.2
Burned						
Burnt	.5	.3	.3	.3	.1	.1
Carbonized	17.4	6.7	2.3	1.3	.5	.3
Calcined	20.4	12.7	2.4	1.0	1.0	.6

Note: * = less than .1 percent.

tively. Although some of the faunal remains from the Trigg site were burned during the postexcavation fire, the resulting burn pattern is quite distinct from bones burned preexcavation. Postexcavation burning appears as a light blackening on the exterior surface accompanied by moderate smoke damage. This distinct pattern allowed these bones to be excluded from the count of modified specimens.

The high number of burned bones at the Crab Orchard site may account in part for the low frequency of gnawed and butchered bones. Chew marks tend to be less visible on burned or poorly preserved bone (Klein and Cruz-Uribe 1984:42). This is likely true for butchery marks as well. Most specimens in the Crab Orchard assemblage were burned to near destruction. This degree of burning is caused by prolonged exposure to intense heat, not by any sort of cooking activity (David 1990). The high frequency of carbonized and calcined specimens (38 percent of NISP) leads me to believe that the Crab Orchard residents incinerated bones as a form of refuse disposal.

There are many other modifying processes that are not readily observed on individual faunal specimens. For example, numerous studies have examined the effect that different screen sizes have on the recovery of animal remains. They have shown, time and time again, that the coarser the screen size the greater the bias is toward the recovery of larger fragments, longer and broader skeletal elements, and bigger taxa (James 1997; Payne 1972, 1975; Shaffer 1992). I discussed in Chapter 2 the differences in recovery methods among the three sites. Excavators at both the Crab Orchard and Hoge sites screened soils through 6 mm mesh hardware, while only 12 mm mesh hardware was employed in the excavation of the Trigg site. If no other taphonomic differences beyond mesh size exist between these assemblages, then average specimen weight should be similar between the Crab Orchard and Hoge sites and somewhat higher at the Trigg site because larger mesh size would allow smaller bones to elude collection. Average weight is actually vastly different between the Crab Orchard (1.6 g) and Hoge (5.8 g) sites, while average specimen weight for the Trigg assemblage (4.3 g) falls below that of the Hoge site (see Table 3.1).

The site with the lowest average specimen weight, Crab Orchard, shows the greatest frequency of unidentified specimens. This is not surprising considering the high frequency of burned specimens. Burned bones break more easily and as a result tend to lose their identifying features more quickly (Stiner et al. 1995:235). Specimens that could not be assigned to a taxonomic class comprise 26 percent of NISP of the Crab Orchard assemblage compared to 2–3 percent of the Hoge and Trigg collections (Table 3.3). This difference appears to be less extreme when the percent of specimen weight per level of identification is considered; however, the proportion of difference that exists between the measures remains similar. Unidentified specimens, both in terms of NISP and weight, are about eight times more frequent at Crab Orchard than at the Trigg site. The effect of larger screen size is evident in the figures for the Trigg site, which shows the greatest proportion of specimens identified to the taxonomic level of order and lower for both NISP (70 percent) and weight (93 percent). Coarser screen size recovers larger specimens. Typically, the larger the specimen the more likely it is to exhibit morphological characteristics that allow it to be identified to a lower taxonomic unit such as genus or species. The percentage of specimens identified to order and lower is similar between the Trigg and Hoge sites for weight (93 percent and 87 percent, respectively), but not for NISP (70 percent and 56 percent, respectively).

The high number of unidentified specimens in the Crab Orchard assemblage may be one factor contributing to the low average specimen weight. To examine this possibility more closely, I compare the average specimen weight for each assemblage by taxonomic level of identification. As seen in Figure 3.1, specimen weight is lowest in each category at the Crab Orchard site. So, while the high proportion of unidentified specimens does lower the average weight for the entire assemblage, specimens identified to order and lower and to class weigh less in the Crab Orchard collection than in the other two assemblages. Overall, the Hoge site exhibits a much greater average weight (8.9 g) for specimens identified to order and lower compared to both the Crab Orchard (3.6 g) and Trigg (5.8 g) sites.

To account for variation in average specimen weight that might stem from differences in the sizes of taxon present in each assemblage, I compare specimen weight within a single species, in this case white-tailed deer. I separate the specimens by the presence and absence of burning to further control for differences among the three assemblages since burned bone tends to be smaller in size than unburned bone (Stiner et al. 1995:235). The data graphed in Figure 3.2 demonstrate that between the Hoge and Trigg sites the average specimen weight of deer for burned (5.1 and 5.5 g) and unburned (10.2 and 9.2 g) specimens is similar, while specimen weight at the Crab Orchard site is about one-half of that in both the burned (2.4 g) and unburned (5.5 g) categories. Because average weight for deer is so similar between the Hoge and Trigg sites it is likely that the difference seen in the average weight for specimens identified to order and lower is a result of differences in the taxon present in each assemblage rather than some other taphonomic factor.

Modern land use is another factor that might be contributing to low average specimen weight at the Crab Orchard site. Agricultural activities such

Table 3.3. Summary of the Fauna by Level of Identification.

Taxonomic Level	Crab Orchard			Hoge			Trigg		
	% NISP (n = 12,540)		% Weight (19,736.8 g)	% NISP (n = 5,564)		% Weight (32,066.8 g)	% NISP (n = 11,525)		% Weight (49,811.5 g)
Order and Lower	31.2		72.0	55.9		87.2	69.6		92.7
Class	42.9		25.0	42.6		12.7	27.3		7.0
Unidentified	25.9		3.0	1.5		.1	3.1		.4

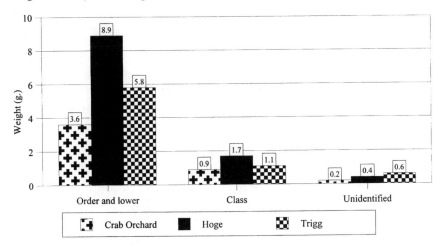

Figure 3.1. Average weight per specimen by level of identification.

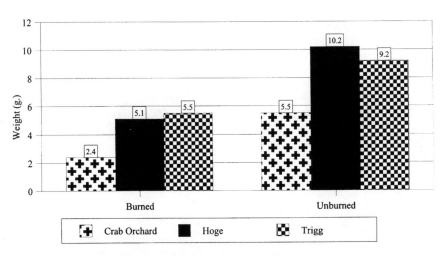

Figure 3.2. Average weight per specimen for white-tailed deer.

as plowing and discing break up faunal remains, which reduces fragment size. Land use at the Crab Orchard site includes farming from historic times up until the early twentieth century (MacCord and Buchanan 1980:3). Unlike specimens recovered from deep within sealed features, materials from surface middens may have been affected by farming activities. Midden contexts comprise about 1 percent of the Crab Orchard assemblage. If historic plowing aided in reducing specimen size, then the average weight per specimen of the midden fauna should be lower than the fauna from feature contexts. This hypothesis is not well supported by the data. Average weight of the midden fauna (1.4 g) is similar to the fauna from storage pits and shallow basin features (1.7 g), which may indicate that the midden deposits were below plow-zone. Hearth contexts produce, by far, the lowest average specimen weight (.4 g), which is not unexpected considering the high frequency of burned bone. The Hoge site, which exhibits the highest average specimen weight, is the only site whose modern land use history excludes farming. Considering that sealed deep-feature contexts comprise 76 percent of the assemblage, the absence of farming activities should have little impact on specimen weight. The data do not follow the expected pattern. Storage pits and burial features, which average 76 cm in depth, actually exhibit a lower average specimen weight (5.6 g) than do hearths, storage structures, and domestic structures (6.7 g), all of which are features that have little depth (6–15 cm) to them.

The taphonomic history of the Crab Orchard assemblage differs in several ways from the Hoge and Trigg collections. It exhibits a greater proportion of burned bone and a lower average specimen weight for both burned and un-burned specimens. In addition, bone preservation was least impressive for this collection. These data lead me to believe that food processing and consumption practices differed somewhat compared to traditions at the Hoge and Trigg sites. The occupants of the Crab Orchard site incinerated bone refuse prior to or following disposal. More intensive bone breakage during processing and consumption or greater trampling of debris are other likely causal factors.

Taxonomic Representation

Each assemblage differs from the other in the frequency of the fauna present, although the degree of difference depends upon the measurement considered. NISP shows greater variability compared to biomass in the proportion of specimens within each class category. As mentioned, the Crab Orchard assemblage contains a much higher proportion of unidentified specimens than either the Hoge or Trigg sites. The Trigg site, in contrast, exhibits a significantly greater number of reptilian specimens, mostly turtle, than the other two assemblages. NISP frequencies are directly related to how the measure reacts to various taxonomic biases. NISP is sensitive to bone fragmentation and tends to overrepresent species with a greater number of skeletal elements or more easily broken or identified bones, such as turtle.

Differences among the three assemblages are less marked in the proportion of biomass. Mammalian taxa comprise between 92 and 95 percent of total

Table 3.4. Summary of Fauna by Taxonomic Class.

	Crab Orchard		Hoge		Trigg	
	% NISP (n = 12,540)	% Biomass (204.8 kg)	% NISP (n = 5,564)	% Biomass (333.4 kg)	% NISP (n = 11,525)	% Biomass (437.4 kg)
Mammals	55.1	94.5	76.4	93.4	52.6	91.8
Birds	4.5	1.5	18.0	5.8	4.9	2.6
Fishes	4.2	.3	.1	*	6.9	2.1
Reptiles	10.2	3.6	3.9	.8	31.5	3.5
Amphibians	.2	n/c	.1	n/c	1.1	n/c
Unidentified	25.9	n/a	1.5	n/a	3.1	n/a

Note: * = less than .1 percent; n/a = not applicable; n/c = not calculated.

biomass at each site. The proportion of birds, fishes, and reptiles vary among the assemblages. I believe biomass provides the best gauge of the relative dietary contribution of different animal species for two reasons. First, biomass estimates are only computed for bones identified to the taxonomic level of class and lower. This helps to even out discrepancies in taphonomic biases that account for the high number of unidentified bones at Crab Orchard compared to the relatively low number at the Hoge and Trigg sites. Second, biomass more appropriately represents certain classes of animals, particularly birds and turtles, because the measure is based on a biological relationship between skeletal weight and animal mass calculated at the class level. For these reasons, I use biomass as the comparative measure in the remaining discussion.

Mammals comprise 92–95 percent of total biomass in each assemblage (Tables 3.4, 3.5). This component consists largely of white-tailed deer (*Odocoileus virginianus*) followed by smaller amounts of black bear (*Ursus americanus*) and wapiti (*Cervus elaphus*). Biomass for each of these taxon varies per site, which I will discuss in more detail in the last section of this chapter. Eight additional mammals are present in all three assemblages: mountain lion (*Puma concolor*), bobcat (*Lynx rufus*), red or gray fox (*Vulpes vulpes, Urocyon cinereoargenteus*), beaver (*Castor canadensis*), woodchuck (*Marmota monax*), raccoon (*Procyon lotor*), eastern cottontail (*Sylvilagus floridanus*), and gray or fox squirrel (*Sciurus carolinensis, Sciurus niger*). Commensals, species such as eastern chipmunk (*Tamias striatus*) and hispid cotton rat (*Sigmodon hispidus*) considered not to have been eaten by site occupants, are also present at each site. The Virginia opossum (*Didelphis virginiana*) is found only at the Crab Orchard site. The Trigg assemblage also contains gray or red wolf (*Canis lupus, Canis rufus*), domestic dog (*Canis lupus*), river otter (*Lontra canadensis*), muskrat (*Ondatra zibethicus*), and striped skunk (*Mephitis mephitis*). Distinctions between wolf and dog are based largely on differences in element size. Measurements for domestic dog fall within the expected range for the region (Guilday 1971; Guilday, Parmalee, and Tanner 1962; Lapham 1998, 2000). All mammals present in the faunal assemblages occupied habitants adjacent to or nearby the villages.

The aves component in each assemblage, which comprises between 3–6 percent of total biomass per site, consists mainly of wild turkey (*Meleagris gallopavo*) (see Tables 3.4, 3.5). A variety of other birds are found in small numbers. Two additional species are present at all three sites: turkey vulture (*Cathartes aura*) and hawk (*Buteo jamaicensis* or *Buteo* spp.). Both species are year-round residents of the Virginia mountains (Virginia Society of Ornithology Checklist Committee 1979:23–25). Four other birds are present at

Table 3.5. Summary of the Fauna by Taxa (Percent of Total).

	Crab Orchard		Hoge		Trigg	
	NISP (n = 12,540)	Biomass (204.8 kg)	NISP (n = 5,564)	Biomass (333.4 kg)	NISP (n = 11,525)	Biomass (437.4 kg)
Cervus elaphus, Wapiti	.3	8.4	1.1	6.0	.3	2.5
Ursus americanus, Black bear	2.2	13.5	2.9	9.7	.6	2.7
Odocoileus virginianus, White-tailed deer	15.2	45.9	38.0	61.9	33.8	75.9
Puma concolor, Mountain lion	*	.3	.1	.8	.1	.2
Lynx rufus, Bobcat	.1	.1	.2	.2	*	.1
Canis lupus/rufus, Gray/red wolf	–	–	–	–	*	.1
Canis lupus, Domestic dog	–	–	–	–	.1	.1
Urocyon cinereoargenteus, Gray fox	–	–	.1	.2	.1	.1
Vulpes vulpes, Red fox	*	*	–	–	*	*
U. cinereoargenteus/V. vulpes, Fox	.1	.1	.3	.1	.2	.2
Castor canadensis, Beaver	*	.2	.3	.7	.3	.5
Lontra canadensis, Northern river otter	–	–	–	–	*	*
Procyon lotor, Raccoon	.1	.1	.5	.3	.7	.7
Didelphis virginiana, Virginia opossum	*	*	–	–	–	–
Marmota monax, Woodchuck	.1	.1	.4	.3	.4	.3
Mephitis mephitis, Striped skunk	–	–	–	–	.1	.1

Continued on the next page

Table 3.5. Continued

	Crab Orchard		Hoge		Trigg	
	NISP (n = 12,540)	Biomass (204.8 kg)	NISP (n = 5,564)	Biomass (333.4 kg)	NISP (n = 11,525)	Biomass (437.4 kg)
Ondatra zibethicus, Muskrat	—	—	*	*	.1	.1
Sylvilagus floridanus, Eastern cottontail	*	*	.2	.1	*	*
Sciurus niger, Fox squirrel	—	—	—	—	.1	.1
Sciurus carolinensis, Gray squirrel	.2	.1	.3	.1	.3	.1
S. niger/carolinensis, Squirrel	.2	*	.1	*	.1	*
Tamias striatus, Eastern chipmunk	.5	n/c	.2	n/c	.1	n/c
Sigmodon hispidus, Hispid cotton rat	.2	n/c	—	n/c	.1	n/c
Microtus pennsylvanicus, Meadow vole	—	n/c	*	n/c	.1	n/c
Peromyscus spp., Mice	*	n/c	—	n/c	*	n/c
Talpidae family, Moles	—	n/c	—	n/c	*	n/c
Rodentia order, Rodents	.3	n/c	*	n/c	.2	n/c
Unidentified very large mammal	*	.2	.3	.5	*	*
Unidentified large mammal	34.7	25.0	30.1	12.3	13.7	7.8
Unidentified medium mammal	.6	.4	1.2	.2	.9	.3
Unidentified small mammal	.1	*	.1	*	.1	*
Meleagris gallopavo, Wild turkey	.8	1.3	7.8	4.4	2.3	2.1
Branta canadensis, Canada goose	*	*	—	—	*	.1

Species						
Haliaeetus leucocephalus, Bald eagle	–	*	–	–	*	*
Ardea herodias, Great blue heron	*	–	–	–	–	–
Phalacrocorax auritus, Double-crested cormorant	–	*	–	–	*	*
Cathartes aura, Turkey vulture	*	*	*	*	*	*
Bubo virginianus, Great horned owl	*	*	–	–	–	–
Corvus corax, Common raven	*	*	*	–	*	*
Buteo jamaicensis, Red-tailed hawk	–	–	.1	.1	–	*
Buteo spp., Hawk	*	*	*	–	.1	*
Bonasa umbellus, Ruffed grouse	–	–	–	.1	–	*
Corvus brachyrhynchos, American crow	.1	.1	–	–	–	*
Podilymbus podiceps, Pied-billed grebe	–	–	–	–	*	–
Colinus virginianus, Northern bobwhite	–	–	–	*	*	*
Scolopax minor, American woodcock	–	*	*	–	*	*
Ectopistes migratorius, Passenger pigeon	–	–	–	.1	*	.1
Anatidae family, Ducks and geese	–	*	.1	–	*	*
Scolopacidae family, Sandpipers	–	–	–	–	*	*
Passeriformes order, Perching birds	*	*	–	–	*	*
Unidentified large/medium bird	4.3	1.4	9.9	1.3	2.2	.4
Unidentified small bird	*	*	–	–	*	*
Pylodictis olivaris, Flathead catfish	–	–	–	–	.5	.2
Ictalurus punctatus, Channel catfish	–	–	–	–	2.0	1.1

Continued on the next page

Table 3.5. Continued

	Crab Orchard		Hoge		Trigg	
	NISP (n = 12,540)	Biomass (204.8 kg)	NISP (n = 5,564)	Biomass (333.4 kg)	NISP (n = 11,525)	Biomass (437.4 kg)
Ictaluridae family, Freshwater catfishes	–	–	–	–	.4	.2
Moxostoma genus, Redhorses	.6	.1	–	–	–	–
Catostomidae family, Suckers	–	–	–	–	*	*
Cyprinidae family, Minnows	*	*	*	*	*	*
Unidentified fish	3.6	.2	.1	*	4.0	.5
Chelydra serpentina, Snapping turtle	–	–	.1	.1	.9	.3
Pseudemys concinna, River cooter	–	–	*	*	.7	.5
Chrysemys picta, Painted turtle	–	–	*	*	*	*
Terrapene carolina, Eastern box turtle	6.4	1.9	2.9	.6	23.8	2.4
Sternotherus odoratus, Common musk turtle	–	–	–	–	.1	*
Unidentified turtle	3.0	.4	.7	.1	3.2	.2
Agkistrodon contortrix, Copperhead	*	*	.1	*	*	*
Viperidae family, Poisonous snakes	–	–	–	–	–	–
Colubridae family, Non-poisonous snakes	*	*	*	*	.2	*
Unidentified snake	*	*	.1	*	2.7	*
Agkistrodon contortrix, Copperhead	*	*	.1	*	*	*
Viperidae family, Poisonous snakes	–	–	–	–	–	–

Colubridae family, Non-poisonous snakes	*	*	*	*	.2	*
Unidentified snake	*	.1	*	*	2.7	*
Cryptobranchus alleganiensis, Hellbender	.1	–	n/c	n/c	–	n/c
Caudata order, Salamanders	–	–	n/c	n/c	*	n/c
Rana catesbeiana, Bullfrog	–	–	n/c	n/c	.1	n/c
Rana spp., Frogs	–	–	n/c	n/c	.3	n/c
Bufo spp., Toads	*	–	n/c	n/c	.1	n/c
Anura order, Frogs and toads	–	–	n/c	n/c	–	n/c
Unidentified amphibian	.1	.1	n/c	n/c	.6	n/c
Unidentified to class	25.9	1.5	n/a	n/a	3.1	n/a

Note: * = less than .1 percent; n/a = not applicable; n/c = not calculated.

two out of three sites: ruffed grouse (*Bonasa umbellus*), American woodcock (*Scolopax minor*), American crow (*Corvus brachyrhynchos*), and Canada goose (*Branta canadensis*). The first three species listed are permanent residents of the study region. Canada goose is a transient and winter visitor (Virginia Society of Ornithology Checklist Committee 1979:12). Present only in the Crab Orchard assemblage are the remains of common raven (*Corvus corax*), great horned owl (*Bubo virginianus*), and great blue heron (*Ardea herodias*). The former two species are year-round residents of the mountain region, while great blue heron is classified as an uncommon permanent resident (Virginia Society of Ornithology Checklist Committee 1979:2, 6, 69). The Trigg assemblage also yields northern bobwhite (*Colinus virginianus*), passenger pigeon (*Ectopistes migratorius*), bald eagle (*Haliaeetus leucocephalus*), and double-crested cormorant (*Phalacrocorax auritus*). The northern bobwhite is a mountain resident. The passenger pigeon, which is now extinct, was once an abundant transient throughout the region. The bald eagle is classified as a rare transient, but this may not have been the case several centuries ago. The double-crested cormorant is also considered to be a rare transient in the southern Ridge and Valley (Virginia Society of Ornithology Checklist Committee 1979:6, 26).

Only two species of fish are present, both in the Trigg assemblage and both catfishes: channel catfish (*Ictalurus punctatus*) and flathead catfish (*Pylodictis olivaris*) (see Table 3.5). Both species are medium- to large-sized catfishes that prefer moderate to deep pools associated with large streams and rivers (Jenkins and Burkhead 1994:537, 568; Stauffer, Boltz, and White 1995:213, 223). Many catfish elements were quite large, ranging from 55 mm to more than 100 mm in length. The Trigg assemblage also yields a hyomandibular bone that belongs to the Catostomidae (suckers) family. Specimens identified to the Cyprinidae (minnows) family are present in very small numbers at all three sites. The Crab Orchard assemblage also contains more than 69 elements identified to the Moxostoma genus (redhorse suckers). The low frequency of fish at the Hoge village likely results from a combination of factors including the proximity of the village to aquatic resources, the capacity of these resources to support aquatic wildlife (both Burkes Garden Creek and Wolf Creek are small streams), and field recovery method. The latter factor would have also biased the recovery of small fish in all three assemblages.

Reptiles comprise between 1 and 4 percent of total biomass in each assemblage (see Table 3.4). All three sites contain large numbers of eastern box turtle (*Terrapene carolina*) (see Table 3.5). The box turtle is a small terrestrial turtle found predominately in open woodlands, although it is also seen in pastures and marshy meadows (Ernst, Barbour, and Lovich 1994:255). John

White, in his watercolor of a box turtle painted in 1585 while he accompanied Walter Raleigh's exploration of the Carolina Outer Banks, described the reptile as "A land Tort which the Savages esteeme above all other Torts" (Hulton 1984:Plate 56). This species may have been a delicacy, as White's characterization suggests, but as its biomass rank indicates box turtles probably did not make a substantial contribution to native diet. Snapping turtle (*Chelydra serpentina*), river cooter (*Pseudemys concinna*), and painted turtle (*Chrysemys picta*) are present in the Hoge and Trigg assemblages. All three species reside in riverine habitats. Like the box turtle, these species are active in the spring and summer and hibernate during the colder winter months (Ernst, Barbour, and Lovich 1994; Mitchell 1994). A fourth aquatic turtle, the common musk turtle (*Sternotherus odoratus*), also known as the stinkpot, is present only at the Trigg site. Turtle meat and eggs are touted to be extraordinary foods with one exception—those from turtles of the "musky" variety (Lefler 1967:138).

Copperhead (*Agkistrodon contortrix*), one of three species of poisonous snakes found in Virginia, is present at all three sites. The copperhead is a terrestrial reptile that occupies a wide range of habitats, most commonly south-southwest facing forested hillsides associated with rock outcrops (Mitchell 1994:288). Native American sentiment toward and uses of venomous snakes varies throughout the Middle Atlantic and Southeast. Certain groups ate Viperidae meat, others did not and viewed the killing of such animals as highly taboo (Ewan and Ewan 1970:374; Lefler 1967:182; Waselkov and Braund 1995:71). Some Native Americans used venomous snakes in medicinal recipes and healing rituals (Lefler 1967:134–135, 227–228). Another species of poisonous snake, the rattlesnake, was regarded to be a clan spirit animal among some Native American peoples (Waselkov and Braund 1995:78, 104–105). A future inquiry focusing on the archaeological context of these copperhead bones may shed light on the use of poisonous snakes in the southern Ridge and Valley.

Amphibian bones are found in small numbers in each assemblage. Biomass is not calculated for amphibians, so this final paragraph will rely on the measure of NISP for comparisons. The highest frequency of amphibian bones occurs at the Trigg site (1 percent). Amphibians are found in much lower numbers in the Hoge (.1 percent) and Crab Orchard (.2 percent) assemblages. Of the 129 amphibian bones identified in the Trigg assemblage, 70 percent came from Feature 578 and 16 percent from Feature 84. It is possible that these two features remained open longer or filled more slowly than other features, which allowed time for a large number of amphibians to crawl into the pit and die. Hellbender (*Cryptobranchus alleganiensis*) is represented by ten vertebrae from several features at the Crab Orchard site. This animal is the largest salamander in North America; some exceed a length of more than 60 cm, but most average 30 to 46 cm in length (Nickerson and Mays 1973). The hellbender is common throughout the Appalachian Mountains from northern Pennsylvania south to Tennessee.

Ridge and Valley Animal Exploitation in a Protohistoric Context

Late Woodland and Protohistoric subsistence practices relied on a limited number of animals to make up the majority of the vertebrate fauna resource base. White-tailed deer, black bear, and wapiti represent the top biomass contributors in each assemblage, followed by wild turkey and eastern box turtle. Many other taxa were exploited on a less frequent basis, including mountain lion, beaver, raccoon, woodchuck, and squirrel, to name a few, along with various birds, fishes, and turtles. This pattern is consistent with the subsistence model defined by Michael B. Barber (M. B. Barber n.d.; Barfield and Barber 1992) for the mountain region of Virginia. He predicted an animal resource base focused largely on deer, a substantial amount of meat supplied by wapiti and black bear, with turkeys and box turtles harvested in significant numbers.

The most noticeable change in southern Ridge and Valley animal exploitation patterns is the greater utilization of white-tailed deer during the Protohistoric period. This increased reliance on deer in relation to other taxa is evident in the proportion of biomass that deer contribute to the diet. Biomass for deer is greatest at the Protohistoric Trigg site at 84 percent of specimens identified to the taxonomic level of order and lower. Both Late Woodland sites contain deer in lesser amounts, 72 percent at Hoge and 64 percent at Crab Orchard (Figure 3.3). This pattern is substantiated by several zooarchaeological measures. Compared to other mammalian taxa, deer are consistently represented in higher proportions in terms of biomass, NISP, MNI, and specimen weight at the Protohistoric Trigg site. Taphonomic biases unique to the Crab Orchard assemblage may be causing deer to be somewhat underrepresented. I suspect that deer biomass is low due to food processing and consumption practices that differed from those observed at the Hoge and Trigg villages. If it were possible to adjust for these biases deer biomass may increase somewhat, but I doubt it would bridge the 20 percent gap that currently exists in deer biomass between the Crab Orchard and Trigg sites.

Although a limited number of taxa contribute the majority of biomass at each site, two very different patterns are apparent in the proportion of biomass contributed by these taxa. In Figure 3.4 I graph the top four or five

Figure 3.3. Distribution of white-tailed deer.

biomass contributors beyond deer: black bear, wapiti, wild turkey, box turtle, and, at the Trigg site, catfish. I exclude deer from this chart because these data are presented in Figure 3.3 and because the predominance of deer over-shadows the patterns seen among the other top biomass contributors. When deer are included in this figure the summed biomass represented by the taxa ranges from 96 to 98 percent of the total biomass of specimens identified to the taxonomic level of order or lower. At the two Late Woodland sites, Crab Orchard and Hoge, the top biomass contributors are heavily skewed toward black bear and wapiti with lesser contributions by wild turkey and box turtle. In contrast, at the Protohistoric Trigg site, each taxon appears in consistently small proportions. The five taxa represented in Figure 3.4c each contribute 3 percent or less of the total biomass of identified specimens. This pattern emphasizes that deer are the single most predominant contributor of biomass to the vertebrate fauna subsistence base during the Protohistoric period.

In addition to the increased use of deer, the exploitation of other fur-bearing animals also increased during the Protohistoric period. Three animals, in particular, represent important secondary trade items: beaver, raccoon, and fox. From a reading of early eighteenth-century documents one can roughly estimate that for every ten deerskins the pelts of three beavers, three raccoons, and two foxes also entered the southern pelt trade (Stine 1990:12–13). In Figure 3.5, I graph the distribution of these three taxa of the total biomass of other small- and medium-sized mammalian specimens identified to order and lower. Biomass for deer, black bear, and wapiti are excluded because their larger size and greater weight overshadows the pat-

(a)

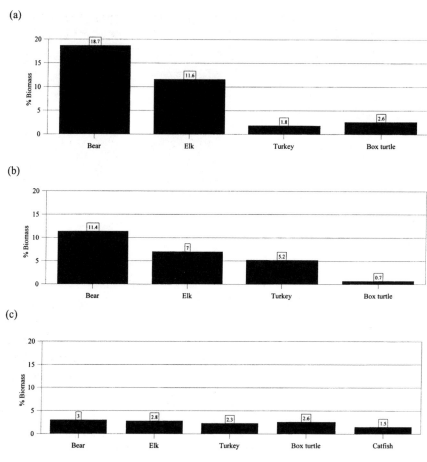

Figure 3.4. Distribution of taxa contributing the most biomass excluding
white-tailed deer, (a) Crab Orchard, (b) Hoge, (c) Trigg.

terns seen among smaller taxa. The proportion of biomass per species differs
by site. Raccoon and fox are present in the highest frequencies at the Trigg
site, while beaver is greatest at the Hoge site. Despite these differences, the
combined biomass for these three fur-bearing animals is greatest at the Protohistoric Trigg site (55 percent) compared to the Late Woodland Crab Orchard
(35 percent) and Hoge (48 percent) sites.

An in-depth examination of the faunal data indicates that several changes
occurred in deer use and subsistence practices during the early to mid-
seventeenth century in the southern Ridge and Valley region of southwestern
Virginia. The exploitation of deer increased substantially, venison gained
greater dietary importance, and the harvest of other fur-bearing animals im-

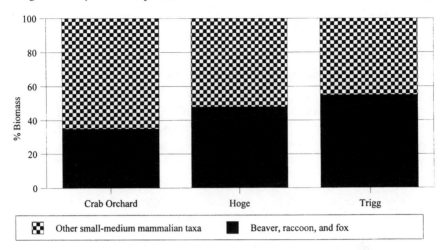

Figure 3.5. Distribution of beaver, raccoon, and fox.

portant to trade increased slightly. The overall breadth of animals contributing to the vertebrate fauna resource base does not appear to decline from
previous times. Instead, subsistence strategies seem to have been adjusted to
incorporate more deer into the economy. This added venison replaced the
meat once provided by other large mammals such as black bear and wapiti.
No ethnohistorical evidence exists to suggest that venison was traded along
with processed hides during this period, although some meat likely entered
exchange systems when hard times fell upon native neighboring groups to
help compensate for local shortages (Rountree 1989:144). Corn, rather than
meat, was the foodstuff most often traded by Native Americans to colonists
(Hatley 1989; Rountree and Davidson 1997:50). It was not until much later
in time and under very different circumstances that venison became an important trade item (see Usner 1992).

The declining use of bear during the Protohistoric period requires further
comment. John Lawson, an Englishman who traveled throughout the Carolinas in the early eighteenth century, refers to bear hunting as a "great sport"
among Native Americans and Euro-Americans alike (Lefler 1967:122). He
recalled being served bear meat on many occasions, describing it as surpass-
ing any meat he had eaten in Europe. Bear fat, he elaborated, was "as white
as snow, and the sweetest of any Creature's in the World" (Lefler 1967:121).
Bear oil was used as a base to turn powdered pigments into paints, in healing
anointments and medicines, and in various feasts and rituals (Lefler 1967:28,
44, 122, 201). Native American peoples also valued bear for its importance in
religion and myth (Hudson 1976:139; Perdue 1998:37–39; Swanton 1946:655–

656; Waselkov and Braund 1995:105). How a decrease in the capture of bear affected these aspects of Native American lifeways can only be speculated upon. It is possible that adjustments were made to ceremonies that incorporated bear or substitute materials found for bear. Rituals that once required the destruction of bear parts may have been altered to spare the item for reuse. Bear may have been killed only when needed for special proposes, although considering the number of times Euro-Americans observed bear being eaten (Lefler 1967:31, 59, 61; Waselkov and Braund 1995:62, 63, 147), this may not have been the case in some regions. It is also possible that bear was reserved for visitors and special occasions, thus giving the appearance that it continued to be a frequent part of native diet throughout the seventeenth century.

4 Deer Hunting and Hide Production

In the previous chapter I presented data on the general composition of the faunal assemblages from the Crab Orchard, Hoge, and Trigg sites. Although venison played an important dietary role at each site, an increase in deer exploitation is evident during the Protohistoric period. In this chapter I examine three specific aspects of deer use: deer hunting strategies, deer butchery practices, and deerskin processing activities. From these perspectives I further define patterns in the animal bone and artifact assemblages that provide additional insights into deer use during the Late Woodland and Protohistoric periods.

Deer Hunting Strategies

Mortality data has been used to examine a wide range of issues, from the origins of animal domestication and the development of specialized animal economies in the Near East (Wattenmaker 1987, 1998; Zeder 1991; Zeder and Hesse 2000) to the selective decision-making and exploitation methods of ancient hunters in Africa and North America (R. Klein 1979; B. Smith 1974; Speth 1983). Kill-off patterns of white-tailed deer are used in this study to investigate whether the deerskin preference patterns that I define in Chapter 1 influenced Protohistoric deer harvest strategies. I have argued that several variables influenced the market value or exchange rate of a deerskin, including the age and sex of the deer, hide size, hide quality, and the degree of processing. Based on the hunting-for-hides model developed in Chapter 1 it is expected that as deerskin production intensified Native American hunters would harvest more prime-age deer, exploit more male than female deer, and kill deer primarily before and after, but not during, molting season. To assess the validity of these assumptions, I examine three variables: age of deer at death, sex of deer hunted, and season of deer kill.

Age of Deer at Death

Age profiles are constructed from analysis of tooth eruption and occlusal wear patterns following C. W. Severinghaus (1949b). To use this method one must first determine the dental formula of the mandible (lower jaw bone).

Deer develop deciduous teeth and replace them with permanent adult teeth in a specific order; the dental formula designates which teeth are present, which in turn allows the mandible to be assigned to one of six age classes. Age determination for the first five age classes (birth to 13 months) is relatively straightforward because age assessment relies primarily on which teeth have or have not erupted and their degree of eruption. Consideration of tooth wear is secondary. By 20 to 24 months of age, deer have replaced their deciduous teeth with permanent teeth and the permanent teeth are fully erupted. Age determination for deer in this and older subclasses relies on identifying patterns of wear to the occlusal surface, lingual and buccal crest and crest dentine, and infundibulum of the mandibular teeth.

Although Severinghaus (1949b) provides detailed and lengthy descriptions of each of the final nine subclasses (20 months to 10+ years of age), his text lacks standardization in the terminology used to describe the different wear stages and a visual representation of these stages. For example, how can one conclusively and consistently distinguish between "slight" wear versus "moderate" or "moderate-to-heavy" wear on the occlusal surface? And, how can one regulate the classification of "narrow" versus "moderate" wear on the lingual crest dentine? These questions, combined with a desire to ensure consistency in my own analysis of more than 150 deer mandibles, led me to develop a point-based ranking system coupled with a series of prototype images that visually represent the different wear stages. I developed this system to standardize how researchers define different stages of wear, not to replace or redefine Severinghaus's existing stages (for further details, see Lapham 2002:Appendix A).

Using these techniques, deer aged younger than 20 months can be accurately assigned to an age class within a two to three month range. Animals older than 24 months are grouped into year classes (i.e., 1 year, 2 year, 3 year, and so forth). When a provenience contained both a right and a left mandible, I examined the two specimens for similarities between occlusal wear patterns and metric data. If it appeared that the mandibles may have belonged to the same animal, I removed one of the two specimens from the sample. More than 20 years ago, Jerry McDonald (1984) aged 97 deer mandibles from the Trigg site using the Severinghaus method. To ensure consistency throughout this study I decided to reexamine these specimens. I had also identified an additional 25 mandibles during my analysis of the general faunal remains from the Trigg site that could be included in the current study. When an assigned age class differed between my own analysis and McDonald's study, a visual comparison of the mandible with specimens from the two possible associated age classes determined its final age. The recommended sample size for constructing age profiles is 25 to 30 mandibles (Lyman 1987b: 140; Klein and Cruz-Uribe 1984:57). This preferred sample size could only be reached for the two Late Woodland sites when the aged samples were combined.

Age profiles exhibit similar distributions at the Crab Orchard ($n = 15$) and Hoge ($n = 18$) sites. Deer aged younger than one year (.5-year age class) comprise the single most prevalent age class followed by animals in the 2.5- and 3.5-year age categories (Figure 4.1a). Late Woodland deer exploitation strategies closely resemble what is called a catastrophic mortality profile. This profile is modeled on the age distribution of animals that occurs when an entire living population is killed in a single catastrophic event (Klein and Cruz-Uribe 1984:56). The resulting distribution is one in which successively older age classes contain progressively fewer animals. The natural structure of a white-tailed deer population also conforms to this distribution (Emerson 1980:122–123). With the exception of the low frequency of animals in the 1.5-year age class, the age composition of deer at the two Late Woodland sites fits well with the catastrophic mortality model.

A very different pattern of deer exploitation is suggested by the age profiles at the Trigg site ($n = 112$) where deer aged to 3.5 years represent the single most prevalent age class followed by other prime-age animals (Figure 4.1b). Unlike the high frequency of juvenile deer noted at the two Late Woodland sites, few animals younger than 1.5 years of age are present in the Protohistoric Trigg assemblage. This type of age distribution is best described as a prime-age dominated mortality profile.

To test the statistical significance of these data, age classes were grouped into three categories based on white-tailed deer maturation and growth: juvenile (.5 years), prime-age (1.5 to 4.5 years), and older adult (5.5 to 8.5+ years). A chi-square test indicates that there is no statistically significant difference in the age of deer at death between the two Late Woodland sites ($\chi^2 = .515$, $df = 2$, $p > .10$). A statistically significant difference does exist, however, in the age of deer hunted between the Late Woodland and Protohistoric periods ($\chi^2 = 5.731$, $df = 2$, $p > .10$). A sample size of less than 40 aged deer mandibles at the Late Woodland sites ($n = 33$) precludes the use of the Kolmogorov-Smirnov to test the goodness-of-fit of these data.

Archaeologists have hypothesized that prime-age dominated mortality profiles can result from any number of factors, including conscious conservation practices that protected fawns (Elder 1965:369), complimentary strategies of deer predation among human hunters and wolves (B. Smith 1974:37,

(a)

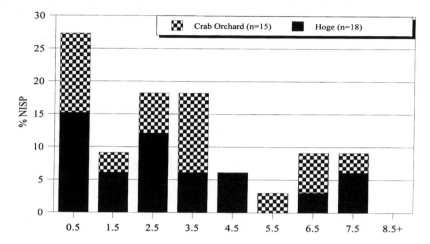

(b)

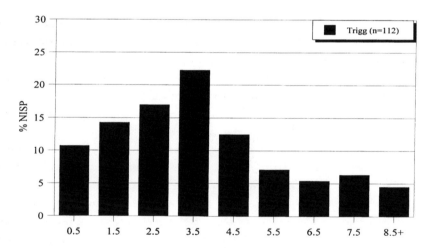

Figure 4.1. Age of deer at death in years, (a) Late Woodland sites, (b) Protohistoric site.

1975:29–31), differential butchering and processing of juvenile animals (Reher 1974:122; Speth 1983:71; Waselkov 1977:115, 1978:21), and differential scavenging by carnivores (Munson 1991; Munson and Garniewicz 2002).

The fourth argument, which maintains that carnivore gnawing causes greater attrition of mandibles from fawns than adult deer because their bones are more fragile, in turn creating an underrepresentation of juvenile animals in archaeological mortality profiles (Munson 1991; Munson and Garniewicz 2002), is not supported by the archaeological data. Of the aged mandibles at the Trigg site, few show signs of carnivore gnawing. Carnivore gnawing is also infrequent in the general faunal assemblage (see Table 3.2). Juvenile animals are said to be better represented when frequencies of individual teeth are calculated because teeth survive better than mandibles (Munson and Garniewicz 2002:414); however, at the Trigg site these data are almost identical. Teeth from juvenile animals (deer 20 months of age and younger) represent 12 percent of all individual teeth, while 15 percent of the aged mandibles belong to juvenile animals. The possibility that differential processing of fawns results in a mortality profile dominated by prime-age animals is not entirely supported by the archaeological data either because deer in the six-month-age class are present at 11 percent of the hunted population.

The hypothesis that Native American hunters had a greater opportunity to harvest middle-aged deer because wolves had killed many of the youngest and oldest, or weakest, animals, cannot be immediately ruled out since wolves have been documented in the study region. The Trigg faunal assemblage contains four wolf bones, three teeth from a single feature and a fairly complete scapula. At most, two animals are represented. Wolf bones are absent from the Crab Orchard and Hoge sites. It is highly unlikely that the wolf population increased in the southern Ridge and Valley between the Late Woodland and Protohistoric periods to the extent that wolf predation caused a significant decline in the number of fawns in the region. Rather, the presence of wolf bones at the Trigg site may represent another example of an animal being hunted for its fur. Wolf skins, like fox and bobcat, were processed in small numbers for commercial trade (Ewan and Ewan 1970:385; Lefler 1967:124; Stine 1990:13; Waselkov and Braund 1995:57).

The premise that Native American hunters avoided killing fawns to allow them to grow into "better hides and more meat" to be used for trade purposes during the historic era (Elder 1965:369) is a reasonable argument when considered within the context of the Protohistoric Trigg site. Fawns have small hides that brought, at best, a minimum exchange rate in the historic deerskin market. Moreover, to ensure a healthy deer population a certain number of fawns must reach reproductive maturity and bear young. Fawns have much lower reproductive rates compared to yearling and adult animals, which decline even further during periods of poor nutrition (Ozoga and Verme 1982:291–294; Verme 1969:882–883) and when population size increases (Xie et al. 1999:124–125). They are also much more likely than older animals to be killed by nonhuman predators, such as wolves, coyotes, and black bears. A recent study of modern fawn survival rates in Pennsylvania demonstrates that by nine months of age between 50 and 60 percent of the fawn population had died, primarily due to predation and other natural causes such as malnutrition and starvation (Vreeland, Diefenbach, and Wallingford 2004). These modern studies demonstrate that fawn mortality is high enough without human hunters, past or present, furthering the death rate.

Sex of Deer Hunted

I determine the sex of deer hunted from an examination of the pelvic bone following a technique developed by Kenneth Edwards and colleagues (1982). The position and shape of the ilio-pectineal eminence (IPE), an elevated feature situated on the pubis portion of the pelvic girdle, differs between male and female deer in animals one year of age and older. In males, the IPE appears as a raised, rounded protuberance positioned above the edge of the acetabular branch of the pubis. In females, the IPE exhibits as a flattened, sharp, shelflike appearance positioned on, rather than above, the edge of the acetabular branch. These morphological characteristics are not fully developed in deer aged younger than 20 months as roughly estimated by the incomplete ossification of the acetabulum.

Before applying this method to the archaeological specimens I conducted a blind test on more than 30 *Odocoileus virginianus* skeletons of known sex. These modern skeletons belong to the Division of Mammals at the Natural Museum of Natural History, Smithsonian Institution. Using the methods outlined by Edwards and colleagues (1982), I accurately determined the sex for 97 percent of the comparative specimens. The one modern specimen that I sexed incorrectly came from a skeleton obtained from the Smithsonian Institution's National Zoological Park. The NMNH catalog lists the skeleton as female, but pelvis characteristics as well as metric data place this animal within male population parameters. Epiphyseal fusion patterns are also unusual.

The sex of deer hunted differed slightly between the two Late Woodland sites, although this may be the result of sample size. At the Crab Orchard site ($n = 7$), female deer are found in a greater frequency than male deer (57 percent to 29 percent, respectively). The Hoge site ($n = 25$) shows an equal proportion of both male and female deer (48 percent each) (Figure 4.2a). Both sites also contain one specimen, likely from animals younger than one year old, that could not be assigned to either the male or female category. Based on modern, nonmanaged white-tailed deer populations the expected male to female ratio is about 50:50 (Emerson 1980:120; McCabe and McCabe 1997:15). Only the Hoge site falls within these expected values. The Crab

(a)

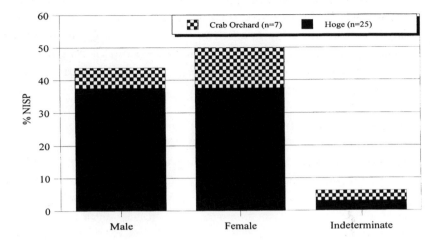

(b)

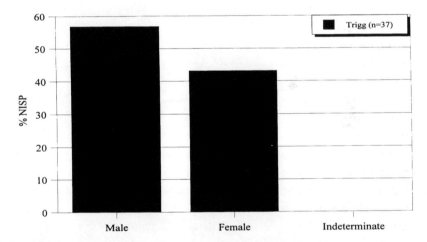

Figure 4.2. Sex of deer hunted, (a) Late Woodland sites, (b) Protohistoric site.

Orchard assemblage is quite small with only six sexed pelvises. I suspect that if sample size increased, the male to female sex ratio would become more equal in its proportions.

All pubic bones at the Trigg site (n = 37) could be designated either male or female based on the development and position of the IPE. The presence of two specimens of indeterminate sex in the Late Woodland assemblages and the absence of such specimens at the Trigg site reflects differences already

observed in the ages of deer killed by Late Woodland and Protohistoric hunters. Both the Crab Orchard and Hoge sites exhibit a greater harvest of juvenile animals, which contrasts with the Trigg site that shows a focus on adult
animals. In comparison to the sex ratios observed at the Crab Orchard and
Hoge sites, male deer outnumber female deer at a ratio of about 60 percent
to 40 percent, respectively (Figure 4.2b). The higher proportion of males
present in the Trigg assemblage also contradicts sex ratios exhibited in many
modern, nonmanaged white-tailed deer populations.

These data suggest that Native American hunters exploited more male
than female deer during the Protohistoric period, although this hypothesis is
not supported statistically. A chi-square test indicates that there is no statistically significant difference in the sex of deer killed between the Late Woodland and Protohistoric periods (χ^2 = .676, df = 1, p > .10). The sex of deer can
also be determined from the presence or absence of antlers on the frontal
bone of the cranium. This index tends to be a less accurate representation
of the sex ratio of deer killed (B. Smith 1975:33) and therefore will not be
used here.

Season of Deer Kill

The season of deer kill is evaluated in two ways. First, for deer aged younger
than 20 months based on mandibular tooth eruption and wear patterns, seasonality is estimated by adding the assigned two- to three-month age range
to the average fawn drop date for the study region of June 1st (McGinnes and
Downing 1973; Severinghaus 1949b). Deer aged older than 20 months are
grouped into less precise age classes that prevents reliable seasonality assessments based on the above method. A second reliable gauge of seasonality is
based on antler development. Male deer grow and shed antlers in annual
cycles. Skulls with antlers attached indicate a May to mid-December death,
whereas skulls with antlers shed signal a late December to March or April
death (Linzey 1998:289; Severinghaus and Cheatum 1956:110).

The Crab Orchard (n = 4) and Hoge (n = 5) assemblages yield only nine
deer mandibles that could be attributed to a season of death. One site exhibits a fall to early winter focus, while the other site displays harvests that range
from late spring to fall (Figure 4.3a). Deer are killed in the lowest numbers
during January, February, and March. The lack of animals procured during
winter and spring may be culturally significant in terms of hunting seasons
or it may be a result of inadequate sample size. Seasonality is also estimated
based on 11 frontal bones from the cranium of male deer, three from the Crab
Orchard site and eight from the Hoge site. All specimens show antlers attached, indicating a May to early December death. These data further sub-

(a)

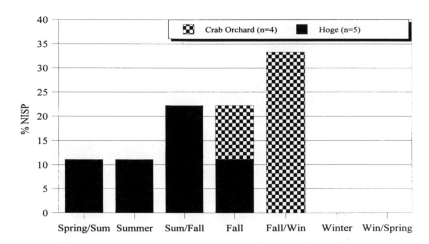

(b)

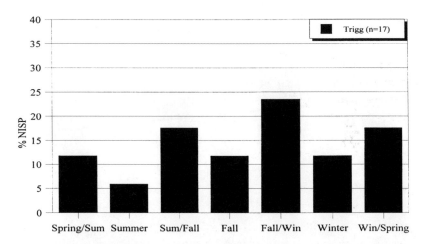

Figure 4.3. Season of deer kill, (a) Late Woodland sites, (b) Protohistoric site.

stantiate the pattern seen in the mandibular seasonality profiles that suggest that deer hunting may not have extended into winter and early spring.

From the Trigg assemblage 17 deer mandibles aged younger than 20 months could be assigned to a season of death. The seasonality profile indicates that deer harvests took place year-round (Figure 4.3b). Deer are killed in the lowest numbers during May, followed closely by July, August, and March. In the study region, deer molting seasons occur in late spring, generally sometime in May or early June, and again in early autumn, sometime in August or early

September (Stüwe 1986:58–60). It is notable that few deer are killed during the main molting months, May and August. I also evaluated season of kill based on five cranium fragments from male deer. Four specimens had the antlers attached, pointing to a May to early December death, and one specimen had the antler shed, indicating a mid-December to April death. These data substantiate the pattern exhibited in the mandibular seasonality profiles, which indicates that during the Protohistoric period deer harvests took place throughout the year.

The mandibular seasonality data suggest that deer harvests became less of a seasonal activity during the Protohistoric period, although this hypothesis is not supported statistically. A chi-square test indicates that there is no statistically significant difference in the season of deer killed between the Late Woodland and Protohistoric periods (χ^2 = 3.340, df = 3, p > .10), however because more than three-fifths of the fitted cells are sparse (frequency > 5) the computed tests are suspect.

Methodological Considerations

The study of deer mortality profiles presented in this study would benefit from three methodological advances. First, as I describe above, greater standardization needs to be applied to the meaning of the terms used to describe the various wear stages that are used to age deer mandibles following the Severinghaus (1949b) method. In an attempt to resolve the inconsistent application of these terms, I developed a point-based ranking system that accompanies prototype drawings of the wear stage for each assessed criteria of wear (see Lapham 2002:Appendix A). The benefits of using this supplement are twofold: (1) it provides a way to standardize mandibular tooth wear assessments and allows for more consistent application of the age class formulas first developed by Severinghaus more than 50 years ago; (2) researchers can more objectively gauge wear stages because each tooth is assessed as a distinct entity and the numerical scores for each tooth carry equal weight. The downside to this system is that, at present, it has not been tested on deer of known age and sex to assess its overall accuracy. Mandibular wear may differ between male and female deer due to differences in feeding behavior and foraging strategies (Van Deelen et al. 2000). The molariform eruption and wear aging method may also be less accurate than previously believed (Hamlin et al. 2000).

Second, a more refined picture of the age-sex structure of deer mortality is needed to more accurately assess the different ages at which hunters killed male and female deer. In the present study, age and sex are calculated from two separate methods, one based on mandibular tooth eruption and wear patterns and the other on the position and shape of the ilio-pectineal eminence. Using these methods a mandible can be aged and a pubic bone can be sexed; however, an animal aged to the 3.5-year age class could be either male or female and a pelvis that has been sexed as male could belong to a deer aged two years, five years, or older. Ideally, in future research, age and sex will be correlated with each other. A recent technique developed by Melinda Zeder (2001; Zeder and Hesse 2000) that combines epiphyseal fusion and metric data to construct sex-specific age profiles for Near Eastern caprines holds much promise for similar work with white-tailed deer populations in North America.

Third, the two measures used to estimate the season of deer kill do not allow for an unequivocal answer to the question of whether Native American hunters harvested deer before and after, but not during, molting season. The fine gauge of seasonality needed to determine precisely where the death falls in relation to molting periods is not fully achieved. Moreover, season of death calculated for animals aged younger than 20 months may or may not provide a reliable assessment of when hunters killed prime-age and older adult deer. Seasonality based on antler development also results in two very broad categories that are useful only as a general gauge as to what time of year hunting took place. Tooth cementum analysis may provide an alternative avenue of study in future research, one that may potentially allow for season of kill to be measured on a more refined level for animals of all ages (e.g., see Landon 1993, Lieberman 1994; Spiess 1990).

Summary

In sum, deer mortality profiles during the Late Woodland period closely resemble the natural structure of a white-tailed deer population in terms of the age and sex of the animals killed. Deer harvests occurred primarily during late summer, fall, and early winter. In contrast, during the Protohistoric period deer kill-off patterns are dominated by prime-age animals, more male than female deer, and deer hunted fairly regularly throughout the year. The significance of deer molt on Protohistoric deer harvests is difficult to assess, however the data hint that hunters procured deer in the lowest numbers during months in which deer molt occurred. Chi-square test results of the statistical significance of the observed age, sex, and seasonality patterns varied and additional data should be collected to confirm or refute the results.

Deerskin Production Activities

I assess deerskin production and production-related activities in several ways. First, butchery marks associated with hide removal are isolated to determine if skinning was performed with the intent of maximizing hide size.

Next, I examine the proportions of deer elements in each assemblage. I then consider the intrasite distribution of skinning marks and body part frequencies indicative of carcass processing to delineate activity areas within each village where initial hide production–related activities may have occurred. Second, I consider the relative frequencies of tools and features used to process deer hides. These data provide another measure of the intensity of hide production activities. I also examine the intrasite distribution of hide processing tools and features to locate where deerskin production may have taken place. I expect that as hide production intensified the frequency of skinning marks will increase and hide processing tools and features will become more numerous.

Carcass Processing

Butchery marks on deer bones provide insight into how people modified and used these ungulates and their various body parts. To examine butchery mark patterns I collected information on the number of butchery events, scar type, the number of scars per butchery event, scar length, orientation and location, and butchery function. A butchery event was defined as discrete if more than one scar occurred on a specimen when the scars were greater than 1 cm apart and nonoverlapping. Butchery scar function follows Binford (1981:Table 4.04), although function can sometimes be ambiguous because scars indicative of a specific function (e.g., skinning, dismemberment, consumption, etc.) often occur in similar locations (Lyman 1987c:264).

Two main types of butchery marks are present on deer specimens from the study sites: cuts, defined as narrow incised lines, and hacks, which appear as slightly deeper, wedge-shaped scars. Scars ranged from less than .5 cm to longer than 1.5 cm in length. The majority (> 85 percent) of deer butchery in each assemblage can be characterized as single event cut marks comprised of five or fewer scars that measure 10 cm or less in length. Scar orientation and location reveals a pattern consistent with butchery practices observed elsewhere in the Middle Atlantic and Southeast (e.g., see Guilday 1971:27–29; Guilday, Parmalee, and Tanner 1962:72–77; Waselkov 1977:87–89).

All skeletal elements exhibit butchery marks, but the single most common scar in all three assemblages are cut marks on tarsal bones. Butchery is present most often on astragali. Scarring also occurs on calcanei, central and fourth tarsals, and a second and third tarsal. Similar cut marks are associated with the dismemberment of the hindfoot from the lower hindlimb (Binford 1981:119). Cuts on the distal humerus, characteristic of dismemberment and filleting, are also common (Binford 1981:124, 131). Overall, less than 5 percent of all deer bones in each assemblage bore butchery scars, with scars intended to sever tendons and ligaments at limb joints predominant. The

Table 4.1. Summary of Deer Butchery.

	Crab Orchard	Hoge	Trigg
Deer NISP	1,910	2,112	3,898
No. of Total Butchered Specimens	20	46	139
No. of Skinning-for-Skin Cuts	–	1	8
Butchery Type			
Cut	15	41	119
Hack	5	5	19
Combination	–	–	1
% Butchered of Deer NISP	1%	2%	4%
% Skinning-for-Skin Cuts of Total Butchered Deer Specimens	–	2%	6%

Trigg site exhibits twice the frequency of butchered deer specimens compared to the Crab Orchard and Hoge sites (Table 4.1). Cut marks made by metal tools, as differentiated by their hairline appearance and bone "shelf" (see Binford 1981:105–106), are not present in the Trigg assemblage although the possibility exists that village residents may have acquired metal-edged tools through trade.

Before muscle and meat can be extracted from a carcass, the hide of the animal must be removed. This distinction between "butchering" and "skinning" is made by several researchers. John Guilday and colleagues (1962) determined that skinning most often began along the distal shaft of the metapodial just above the dew-claws. The process occasionally cut lower on the foot, scarring the phalanges and distal epiphysis of the metapodial (Guilday, Parmalee, and Tanner 1962:73). The Eschelman site, where this pattern was observed, is part of the Protohistoric period Susquehannock Washington Boro village complex located along the Susquehannock River in south-central Pennsylvania. Numerous European-manufactured goods were recovered from the village, including iron knives, axes, hoes, metal projectile points, four whole kettles, a brass spoon, numerous copper-alloy ornaments and hawk-bells, and more than 7,000 glass beads (Kent 1984). Historical accounts document the Susquehannock's extensive participation and influence in the region's deer and beaver pelt trade (Fausz 1985:250; Kent 1984:34–35).

Another distinction in butchery patterns has been made between "skinning" and "skinning-for-skins." Lewis Binford (1981), in his landmark study of animal bone modifications, observed that in certain circumstances skinning-for-skins differed from skinning as a stage of butchery. When processing meat was the primary objective among the Alaskan Nunamiut, skinning often began with a cut encircling the proximal metapodial or sometimes the associated distal lower limb bone (i.e., radius/ulna and tibia). During late summer and early fall caribou hunts, when the skins of yearlings and calves were desired for use in the manufacture of clothing, butchers took greater care to begin skinning at the hoof of the animal to ensure that the proper hide shape was obtained for making skin boots (Binford 1981:103). Skinning lower down on the leg would also maximize the size of the hide removed intact from the animal.

Skinning marks, and butchery marks in general, are usually scarce in an assemblage since hide removal and carcass dismemberment can be done without scarring bone (Binford 1978:480; Frison 1970:10–11; Guilday et al. 1962:64). Nevertheless, examining the frequency of skinning scars can provide additional information on hide processing activities. I define skinning-for-skins as localized cut marks found on the lower jaw, on the skull encircling the antlers, and on the distal metapodials and phalanges (Figure 4.4). Scars characteristic of skinning-for-skins are absent in the Crab Orchard assemblage and only one example of a scarred distal metacarpal is present at the Hoge site. Skinning marks are much more prevalent during the Protohistoric period. Mandibles, distal metapodials, and phalanges exhibit skinning scars at a greater proportion at the Trigg site (6 percent) than at the two Late Woodland sites combined (2 percent total) (Table 4.1). Eight storage pits at the Trigg site contain deer bone butchered in a manner consistent with skinning to maximize hide size (Features 71, 83, 169, 221, 277, 345, 483, and 514). These features are dispersed throughout the village (Figure 4.5).

Carcass processing areas are further delineated from a comparison of the proportion of deer skeletal elements at each site. These data in turn allow for the identification of features that contain a high proportion of butchery waste compared to meat-bearing limb elements. To examine element frequencies I divide the deer skeleton into four main body part categories: head (skull, mandible, and hyoid), axial (vertebra, ribs, and sternum), limb (scapula, humerus, radius, ulna, pelvis, femur, patella, and tibia), and foot (carpals, tarsals, metacarpals, metatarsals, and phalanges). Antler has been excluded from these calculations because shed antlers may have been gathered by Native American peoples for use in tool production, which would result in their overrepresentation in the archaeological record. Deer body part dis-

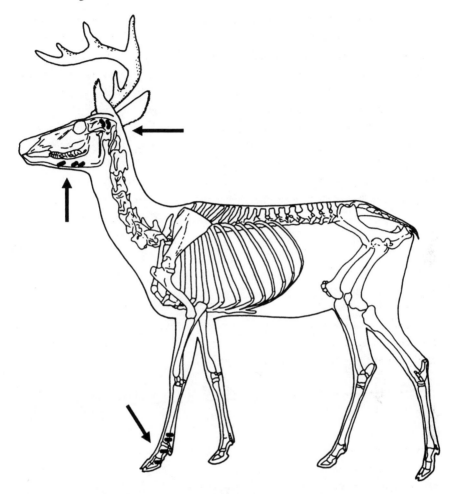

Figure 4.4. General location of cut marks characteristic of skinning scars. Drawing adapted from Reitz and Wing 1999:Figure 7.22.

tributions are almost identical between the Crab Orchard and Trigg sites. Axial and limb elements comprise 53 percent and 57 percent of total biomass for deer of the respective assemblages, while head and feet elements account for the remaining percentages (Figure 4.6). The Hoge site, although similar, shows a greater proportion of axial and limb elements (68 percent) and a lower proportion of head and foot elements (32 percent).

To compare deer biomass even further, I divide the elements into meat-bearing limbs (all elements in limb category, except the patella) and butchery waste (all elements in the head and foot categories, except carpals and tar-

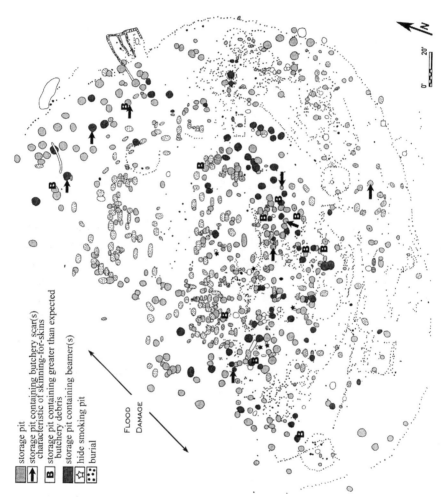

Figure 4.5. Features associated with hide skinning and processing at the Trigg site.

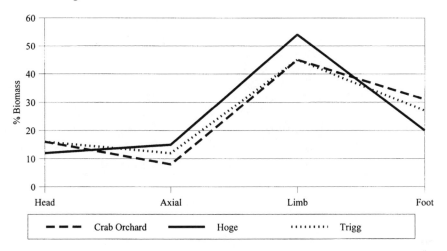

Figure 4.6. Distribution of deer body parts.

sals). Carpals and tarsals are excluded from these calculations because they articulate proximally with lower limb elements and distally with upper foot elements. They could have been transported with either meat-bearing limbs or butchery waste elements, hence the term "riders" (Binford 1981:272). The Crab Orchard and Trigg sites contain meat-bearing limbs and butchery discard in almost identical proportions. Meat-bearing limbs account for 57 percent and 61 percent of deer biomass of the respective assemblages, while butchery waste is present at 43 percent and 39 percent, respectively (Figure 4.7). The Hoge site, in contrast, exhibits a greater proportion of meat-bearing limb bones (71 percent) and a lower proportion of butchery discard (29 percent). One explanation for this pattern may be that residents butchered deer at the kill site to decrease the weight transported back to the village. The Hoge site is located in a remote mountaintop valley that measures about 16 km long by 7 km wide. It is surrounded by ridges that rise an additional 152 to 457 m above sea level, except for a narrow water gap along the northwestern mountain wall. Deer killed beyond the confines of the valley floor would have required much labor to bring back to the village. Butchering the deer prior to transport and leaving behind the less valuable waste elements would have lightened the load carried back to the village.

To identify areas where initial carcass processing may have taken place I examine the spatial distributions of features that contain butchery waste in greater-than-expected proportions. I define greater-than-expected as proportions equal to or greater than 10 percent above the site average. To be included in this comparison a feature had to have an NISP of 20 or greater and

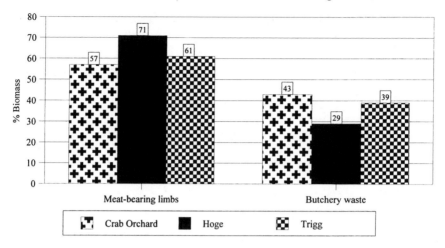

Figure 4.7. Distribution of meat-bearing limbs and butchery waste.

a biomass of 20.0 g or more. There are three features (Features 507A, 512F, and 517C) at the Crab Orchard site that contain greater-than-expected proportions (≥ 53 percent) of butchery debris. These features are distributed throughout the site. Two are storage pits; one is located within a domestic structure, the other is located in the cluster of features northeast of the semisubterranean structure. The third feature is a hearth associated with the semisubterranean structure. The Hoge site yields four features (Features 13, 114, 153, and 184) that contain greater-than-expected proportions (≥ 39 percent) of butchery debris. Two features are storage pits, one is a hearth, and one is a storage structure. The features are scattered across the site. At the Trigg site there are 11 features (Features 71, 197, 210, 283, 341, 352, 369, 451, 454, 456, and 559) that contain greater than expected proportions (≥ 49 percent) of butchery debris. Once again, the features are well distributed throughout the village (see Figure 4.5).

Hide Processing

John Lawson, an Englishman who traveled widely throughout the interior regions of the Carolinas in the early eighteenth century, provides us with one of the most detailed accounts of southeastern Native American hide processing,

Their Way of dressing their Skins is by soaking them in Water, so they get the Hair off, with an Instrument made of the Bone of a Deer's Foot; yet some use a sort of Iron Drawing-Knife, which they purchase of the *English,* and after the Hair is off, they dissolve Deer Brains, (which beforehand are made in a

Cake and baked in the Embers) in a Bowl of Water, so soak the Skins therein, till the Brains have suck'd up the Water; then they dry it gently, and keep working it with an Oyster-Shell, or some such thing, to scrape withal, till it is dry, whereby it becomes soft and pliable. Yet these so dress'd will not endure wet, but become hard thereby; which to prevent, they either cure them in smoke, or tan them with Bark [Lefler 1967:217].

Lawson describes three important aspects of hide processing that survive in the archaeological record. The tool he calls the "Bone of a Deer's Foot" is known as a beamer. Hide-workers used these tools to scrape and clean skins. Beamers were commonly manufactured from a deer metatarsal (upper hind-foot bone) by removing a long, curved, concave section of bone from the central shaft. A hide-worker grasped the tool on either end and drew it across a stretched hide to remove hair, tissue, and fat deposits. Lawson also observed that an "Oyster-Shell" was used to work hides. These mussel shell tools had notched or ground edges to facilitate scraping. In contrast to beamers and mussel scrapers, which were used in the earlier stages of hide processing, hides cured with smoke represent the final phase in hide production. A shallow hole was dug in the ground and filled with slow-burning wood or corn-cobs that smoked rather than flamed. The hide was then hung in a conelike fashion above the pit and left to absorb the smoke. As I described in Chapter 1 and as Lawson alludes to above, smoking had several benefits. It gave the hide a water-resistant quality and made it more resistant to attack by pests. To measure the intensity of hide production activities I consider the relative frequencies and spatial distribution of bone beamers, mussel shell scrapers, and smoking pits.

My analysis of the Crab Orchard faunal remains identified one fragment of the central shaft of a deer metatarsal beamer from Feature 507A. In addition, other functional bone tools recovered during the 1978 excavations include: eight awl fragments and one wapiti antler hoe (Table 4.2). This information combines data from my analysis of the vertebrate fauna and the Virginia Department of Historic Resources specimen catalog records.

The Hoge site yields 20 beamer fragments, six from feature contexts and 14 from midden refuse (Jones and MacCord 2001:164). A leg bone from a large bird was also identified as a beamer, however this tool likely had another function. Removing hair from deer hides is an extremely tough task for which bird bones would not be well suited. Seven fragments of worked deer antler were also identified as "fleshing" tools (Jones and MacCord 2001:164). Fleshers function similar to beamers, however they differ in form. These tools are manufactured from flat bones, usually deer or elk antler or scapula (shoulder

Table 4.2. Summary of the Bone and Antler Tool Assemblages.

	Crab Orchard (*n* = 10)	Hoge (*n* = 133)	Trigg (*n* = 447)
No. of Beamers	1	21	126
No. of Other Tools	9	112	321
Other Tool Types	awl, hoe	awl, fishhook, flesher/hoe, punch, knife, misc. antler tools	awl, fishhook, flaker, chisel, shuttle, needle, projectile point, gouge, hoe
% Beamers of Total Tools	10%	16%	28%
No. of Fishhooks	0	2	36
% of Beamers of Total Tools, Excluding Fishhooks	10%	16%	31%

blade). The working edge is located only on one end similar to an adze. These so-called antler fleshers may have been used as hoes or digging tools since elsewhere similar artifacts have been described as serving this function (e.g., see Barber 2003:196; Egloff and Reed 1980:146). Other functional tools include 92 awls, two fishhooks, four punches, one knife, and three miscellaneous antler tools (Jones and MacCord 2001:164). In addition, my analysis of the Hoge faunal assemblage identified one deer metatarsal beamer fragment and two bird bone awl tips.

To determine the type and number of bone and antler tools at the Trigg site I reviewed feature artifact inventories reported in Buchanan (1984). My survey found 126 beamers along with 188 awls, 48 flakers, 36 fishhooks, 33 chisels, five shuttles or needles, four projectile points, three gouges, three digging tools or hoes, and one miscellaneous bone tool (Table 4.2 and Figure 4.8). Barber (2003) provides additional details on beamer manufacture and use at the Trigg site in a recent study of worked bone and antler artifacts from southwestern Virginia. Most beamers recovered from the Trigg site were produced from deer metatarsal bones; however, two beamers manufactured from deer metacarpals, one from a deer femur, one from a bear humerus,

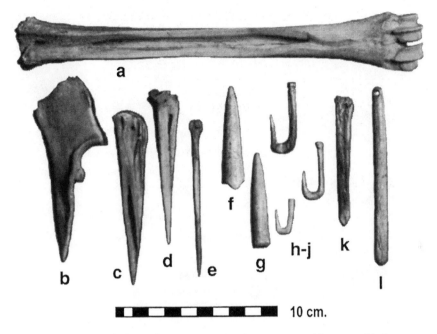

Figure 4.8. Bone tools from the Trigg site, (a) deer metatarsal beamer, (b) deer ulna awl, (c–d) turkey tarsometatarsal awls, (e) raccoon fibula awl, (f–g) antler tine projectile points (h–j) fishhooks, (k–l) blunt end tools.

and one from a bear tibia were also present. Beamers were identified in all stages of production and use, including tools in preparation for use, tools with little or no wear, beamers with midsections thinned, some worn close to the point of exhaustion, and some worn to the point of being broken in use (Figure 4.9). A few beamers also showed evidence of having been re-sharpened through flaking.

At the Crab Orchard and Hoge sites beamers comprise 10 percent and 16 percent the respective bone and antler tool assemblages. This proportion increases to 28 percent at the Trigg site (Table 4.2). The faunal data that I present in Chapter 3 indicates that fish contribute very little to the diet of the Crab Orchard and Hoge site residents, while the Trigg site occupants utilized fish, especially catfish, in much greater quantities. Catfish contributes about 3 percent of biomass to the vertebrate fauna subsistence base, which is comparable to the proportion of biomass contributed by the four other secondary taxa (black bear, wapiti, wild turkey, and box turtle; see Figure 3.4c). If the bias created by the presence of fishhooks is eliminated, the proportion of

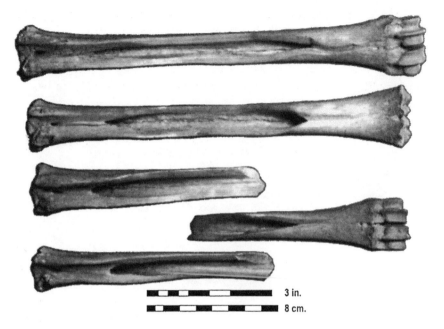

3 in.

8 cm.

Figure 4.9. Deer metatarsal beamers from the Trigg site showing various stages of use wear.

beamers at the Trigg site increases to 31 percent of the total bone and antler tool assemblage, a frequency almost double that seen at the Late Woodland sites. A chi-square test indicates that there is no statistically significant difference at the two Late Woodland sites in the number of beamers compared to other bone and antler tools (χ^2 = .011, df = 1, p > .01). Despite the bias created by fishhooks, a chi-square test corroborates that there is a statistically significant difference in the number of beamers relative to other bone tools between the Late Woodland and Protohistoric periods (χ^2 = 8.797, df = 1, p > .01).

To determine if areas of more intense hide processing existed within each village I plot the spatial distribution of beamers by feature. The one beamer fragment identified at Crab Orchard came from the upper fill of Feature 507A, a large storage pit located within the southernmost house structure. Unfortunately, provenience information is not available for bone tools from the Hoge site. At the Trigg site, beamers are present in 80 storage pits (Features 66, 69, 74, 77, 83, 84, 90, 104, 110, 113, 117, 127, 158, 191, 192, 201, 202, 204, 211, 212, 215, 218, 232, 247, 273, 274, 277, 283, 292, 299, 302, 303, 313,

320, 321, 323, 325, 326, 338, 342, 358, 359, 365, 366, 371, 406, 415, 420, 439, 442, 456, 471, 473, 481, 493, 496, 502, 503, 507, 510, 512, 514, 522, 526, 537, 549, 553, 559, 572, 578, 597, 598, 617, 624, 629, 638, 640, 666, 713, and 756). These features are scattered across the settlement, but appear to be more heavily concentrated in pits located inside the inner palisade in the southeastern quadrant of the village (see Figure 4.5). A cache of beamers was found near the base of Feature 572 (Buchanan 1984:204) and a beamer in the initial preparation stage of manufacture was recovered from Feature 526 (M. B. Barber 2003).

Information on mussel shell scrapers reveals additional information on hide processing at the Hoge and Trigg sites; data on these artifacts at the Crab Orchard site has not yet been published. Three scrapers out of 915 total mussel shells were identified at the Hoge site, two *Cyclonaias* sp. (likely purple wartyback, *Cyclonaias tuberculata*) and one *Elliptio* spp. (either *E. crassidens*, elephant-ear, or *E. dilatata*, spike) (Jones and MacCord 2001:175). *Elliptio* spp. are predominant at 98 percent of the total mussel assemblage. Both elephant-ear and spike mussels could have been procured from nearby Wolf Creek, while the purple wartyback was likely collected from the New River and brought into the valley by village residents. At the Hoge site, scrapers comprise less than 1 percent of the total mussel shell assemblage (Table 4.3).

At the Trigg site, excavators saved only a sample of the freshwater mussels recovered (Buchanan 1984:322); it is unknown how many specimens were tossed. Of the 334 mussels collected two species were present, purple wartyback (68 percent) and elephant-ear (32 percent) (Table 4.3). Modification patterns display a clear preference for purple wartyback mussel scrapers to exhibit notched-edges (73 percent) and for elephant-ear scrapers to show ground-edges (97 percent). These two species have very different shapes, which likely influenced function and use. The purple wartyback has a more circular shape to it, while the elephant-ear is elliptical with a flattened ventral edge (Parmalee and Bogan 1998:69, 77). With its ground ventral edge, an elephant-ear scraper would function much like a bone beamer. The notched edges of the purple wartyback scraper may have been useful in loosening fleshy debris or breaking down course fibers to soften a hide. I can only speculate, however, as to whether or not both types of shell scrapers were used in hide processing. In total, 83 percent of the collected mussels were modified for use as scrapers at the Trigg site. Provenience information is unavailable for these artifacts.

Smoking pits, also called smudge pits, have been identified in many archaeological contexts as small, oval-shaped features filled with carbonized or-

Table 4.3. Summary of the Freshwater Mussel Assemblages.

	Hoge ($n = 915$)	Trigg ($n = 334$)
Total *Cyclonaias* sp.	20	228
No. of Notched-edge Scrapers	1	166
No. of Ground-edge Scrapers	1	6
Total *Elliptio* spp.	895	106
No. of Notched-edge Scrapers	1	2
No. of Ground-edge Scrapers	–	103
% Scrapers of All Mussels	*	83%

* = less than 1 percent.

ganic materials, typically corncobs (Binford 1967). In this study I define smoking features as "small pits (under 46 cm in diameter with about the same depth) filled with burned corncob fragments, twigs, bark, or a combination of the these" (Buchanan 1984:5). Such features are absent in the 1978 excavation area at Crab Orchard site (Egloff and Reed 1980), although other areas of the village yielded three possible smoking pits (Features 68, 77, and 224) (MacCord and Buchanan 1980). Smoking pits are also absent at the Hoge site (Jones and MacCord 2001:133).

At the Trigg site, four definite (Features 449, 450, 542, and 582) and one probable (Feature 620) smoking pits are present (Buchanan 1984). Four of these features are located in the northeast section of the southwest quadrant of the village and one is located in the adjoining corner of the northeast quadrant (see Figure 4.5). In general, smoking pits are few in number, possibly because this part of the production process is a hot, smoky task. Hides may have been smoked outside of the main activity areas, beyond the palisade walls. Two other explanations exist for the low numbers of smoking pits. As deerskin production for trade intensified, it is possible that hides were no longer smoked or perhaps the method of smoking changed in order to accommodate more hides. If hides were smoked in mass rather than in small numbers over individual fires, whatever new types of features resulted from these activities may be unrecognizable as such in the archaeological record. Rather than smoking a single hide over a pit, multiple hides may have been smoked inside a structure specifically designed for this purpose such as the hide smokehouses used among the Blackfoot (Ewers 1945:12).

Summary

In sum, several lines of evidence linked to hide-working point to an intensification in deerskin production activities during the Protohistoric period. Cut marks consistent with skinning to maximize hide size become more frequent and bone beamers, mussel shell scrapers, and smoking pits become more numerous. Skinning and initial carcass processing took place in association with households throughout the village (see Figure 4.5). The spatial distribution data suggest a similar pattern at the two Late Woodland sites, although sample size is small.

Deer Hunting and Hide Production in a Protohistoric Context

Economic intensification associated initially with a change from deer procurement for local consumption to deer harvest for commercial trade resulted in more selective predation by Native American hunters in the southern Ridge and Valley. This change reveals that a shift had occurred from a more opportunistic deer procurement practice during the Late Woodland period to a hunting strategy in the Protohistoric period that at times selected for prime-age deer, especially male deer. Deer exploitation may have also broadened from a seasonal activity to year-round harvesting scheduled to avoid killing deer in molt, although evidence for shifting seasons of deer harvests requires further study. In the context of the hunting-for-hides model proposed in Chapter 1 such changes indicate that some native hunters developed selective harvest strategies that focused on procuring animals whose hides would bring the most competitive exchange rates on the commercial market.

Certain aspects of the hunting-for-hides model also provide a good fit with deer harvest patterns seen at other Protohistoric sites in the greater Middle Atlantic region. At the Eschelman site (36LA12), kill-off patterns indicate a focus on prime-age deer (Guilday, Parmalee, and Tanner 1962). Deer harvests occurred most frequently during the fall and winter months, with bucks killed in greater numbers than does (Guilday, Parmalee, and Tanner 1962:62). The Eschelman site, which I previously discussed in the context of deer skinning, is part of a Protohistoric Susquehannock village complex in south-central Pennsylvania. Archaeologists recovered an abundance of European-manufactured goods. Seventeenth-century documents describe a lucrative commerce existing between the Susquehannocks and English fur

traders residing at Kent and Palmer Islands near the mouth of the Susquehannock River in the northern Chesapeake Bay (Fausz 1983:19–20, 1985:250–
251; Kent 1984:34–35).

Native American hunters display a similar preference for harvesting prime-
age deer at the mid- to late seventeenth-century Graham-White site (44RN21)
(Moore and Lapham 1997), a settlement located along the Roanoke River
less than 64 km northeast of the Trigg site. The sex of deer hunted and season
of deer kill has not been assessed, so whether or not deer harvest strategies
were influenced by other factors related to deerskin preference patterns is
uncertain. European artifacts recovered from the site include a trigger from
an English-manufactured snaphaunce firearm, more than 100 glass beads,
several copper-alloy beads and pendants, numerous copper-alloy and iron
sheet fragments, and several iron fragments of indeterminate form (Thomas
Klatka 2004, personal communication). By the time Native American peoples
settled the Graham-White site, the trade and commercial export of deerskins had become one the fastest growing industries in the southern colonies
(J. Martin 1994:310).

In making these comparisons, I am not suggesting that selective deer harvests should be equated unequivocally with a Protohistoric hunting strategy,
nor that this exploitation pattern becomes the norm following European
settlement in the Americas. Where and when selective predation does occur
is especially important. Numerous deer inhabited western Virginia in the
seventeenth century. These areas, which include the western Piedmont, Blue
Ridge Mountains, and Ridge and Valley regions, also yielded some of the
largest deer in the state (Tyler 1907:108; Waselkov and Braund 1995:59). Colonial expansion and increased settlement density in coastal regions coupled
with overhunting led to a reduction in white-tailed deer populations in eastern portions of the state by the early- to mid-eighteenth century (Braund
1993:69; Knox 1997:27–28). Selective deer harvests may represent a hunting
strategy seen primarily during the initial decades of the deerskin trade at a
time when Native American hunters had the luxury of targeting deer whose
hides would bring the most competitive exchange rates. As deer herds continued to decline and competition for good hunting grounds increased, it
may have been more effective for hunters to kill the first available deer regardless of whether or not its hide would bring a high market value.

When selective deer harvests, such as those seen at the Protohistoric Trigg
site, are considered from a regional perspective, it becomes apparent that not
all Native American hunters chose to adopt this predation strategy. At the
Protohistoric Hurt Powers Plant site (44PY144), for example, zooarchaeological data provides no evidence that the deerskin trade influenced deer hunting

strategies, at least not in ways predicted by the hunting-for-hides model. To the contrary, hunters continued to harvest deer as they had in the past. Deer mortality profiles closely resemble the natural age structure of a white-tailed deer population, with harvests occurring primarily during summer, fall, and early winter (M. B. Barber, M. F. Barber, and Bowen 1996:280–281). These data parallel the age and seasonality profiles seen at the Late Woodland Crab Orchard and Hoge sites. Proportions of hide-working tools and features also appear more similar to the Late Woodland period patterns. The Hurt Powers Plant site, which is located along the Staunton River about 113 km directly east of the Trigg site, was occupied sometime during the first half of the seventeenth century. European goods recovered from the site include more than 225 glass beads, 59 copper-alloy beads, pendants and scrap sheet fragments, and an iron knife fragment (M. B. Barber, M. F. Barber, and Bowen 1996). Clearly, occupants of the site had contact with European traders or with native groups who had access to European goods; the latter is more likely given the occupation dates and location of the site. Despite evidence of European goods acquired through exchange or gift-giving, none of the economic changes associated with deer exploitation for commercial trade have been identified in the Hurt Powers Plant assemblage.

This regional perspective suggests that some Native American communities either did not participate in the deerskin trade or participated to a lesser degree than did their neighbors. Whether this was a conscious decision or a matter beyond their control is not known; both scenarios are possible. Certain villages may have chosen not to produce deerskins for trade, for any number of reasons. It is also possible that other Native American groups actively sought to control and even limit who participated in the trade. The Siouan-speaking Occaneechi are well known for their intimidation tactics toward neighboring native groups as they fought to secure and maintain their position as middlemen in the trade. They exerted tight control over important trade routes as well as native access to European traders and their goods, restricting direct contact between western groups and colonial merchants for many years (Ward and Davis 1993:427–428). From their strategically placed villages along the Roanoke River in the central Piedmont of southern Virginia and northern North Carolina, the Occaneechi were also able to dictate which European goods filtered in to interior regions, keeping many of the most valued items, such as guns and iron knives, for their own use. The Occaneechi maintained their key position in the deerskin trade until Nathaniel Bacon and his militia attacked them in 1676 (Ward and Davis 1993:430). With too few Occaneechi remaining to adequately defend their stronghold, they moved south to the Eno River in North Carolina.

Along with selective deer harvests, hide production activities also intensified during the Protohistoric period, at least within some Native American communities. Productive intensification allowed surplus deerskins to be amassed for trade. The question of where production intensified is a difficult one to answer, however. Did only certain households intensify deerskin production? Did processing intensify village-wide? During the Late Woodland period, hide processing occurred at the household level, as it was a necessary task to fulfill basic needs for clothing and shelter. The spatial distribution of skinning marks, butchery waste, hide-working tools, and features at the Trigg site suggests that hide processing took place within most, and likely all, households during the Protohistoric period as well, which makes identifying specific locales of intensified hide production difficult. It appears that hide production intensified village-wide during the Protohistoric period, although this observation is based on negative evidence since no specialized activity areas associated with intensified hide processing could be detected within the Trigg village. Future research may benefit from quantitative spatial analyses that can identify areas of high and low activity through objective and replicable methods.

5   Mortuary Practices and Prestige Goods Use

As evidenced by the data presented in the previous two chapters, certain seventeenth-century Native American communities in the southern Ridge and Valley chose to intensify deerskin production and related activities in order to participate in a growing interregional trade in hides, furs, and non-local goods. In the southern Ridge and Valley, surplus deerskins provided the material means to obtain valued, nonlocal materials that conveyed individual and household wealth, prestige, and power to others within the community. Because most nonlocal goods are found in association with human remains my analysis focuses on mortuary assemblages to better understand cultural change and continuity related to deerskin production and trade in the Proto-historic period. In the following chapter, I first consider general mortuary practices during the Late Woodland and Protohistoric periods, after which I examine the distribution of nonlocal materials, specifically marine shell, cop-per and copper-alloy, and glass. Together, these data provide information on how nonlocal, status-marking goods were used, as well as on the kinds of mortuary contexts in which such items were deposited.

My interest in the use of nonlocal materials in mortuary contexts must be prefaced with the acknowledgment that decisions to bury these items with certain individuals were made by living persons. These decisions may have been related to the statuses held by the deceased in life, the status of the deceased as being among the dead and ancestors, the collective social stand-ing of the family and kin of the deceased, or the status of the people making the deposit (O'Shea 1996:10). The material goods selected for inclusion in the grave could have been personal possessions of the deceased, gifts given to the deceased upon burial by immediate family or kin, or gifts given to the de-ceased upon burial by non-kin relations. To this end, funerary rituals convey as much information about the qualities of the deceased as they do about the interests and aspirations of the mourners (Brown 1995:20–21; Hutchinson and Aragon 2002; O'Shea 1996:13).

One note before I proceed with my analysis. I have chosen to exclude the mortuary data from the Hoge site from the following discussion due to nu-merous problems with the data. These problems can be summarized as: (1) burials looted prior to excavation, (2) burials and associated goods poorly described during excavation, (3) grave goods lost postexcavation, and (4) provenience information lost postexcavation. Boyd and Boyd (2001) found similar inconsistencies with the Hoge site mortuary data in their analysis of the human remains. In order to deal with these inconsistencies they adopted an ossuary methodology in their analysis that eliminated a need for burial context and ultimately provided a broad picture of health and demography at the Hoge village. Because I am interested generally in mortuary practices and specifically in grave good assemblages, the problems with the Hoge site burial data cannot be resolved by a change in strategy. I therefore elected to eliminate the Hoge data from my discussion of mortuary practices and prestige goods use.

General Mortuary Patterns

The 1971–74 field seasons at the Crab Orchard site identified 163 burial features containing 168 individuals (MacCord and Buchanan 1980:80–102). Five burials contained two individuals within a single grave. Douglas Ubelaker in the Division of Physical Anthropology at the Smithsonian Institution's National Museum of Natural History in Washington, D.C., supervised the analysis of the human remains (MacCord and Buchanan 1980:80). The 1978 excavations at the Crab Orchard site yielded an additional 16 burial features from areas both in and around domestic structures as well as outside the palisade (Egloff and Reed 1980:142–145). Three graves contained the remains of two individuals and one burial feature was empty. Combining the burial data from both periods of excavation, the Crab Orchard site yields 179 burials containing 186 individuals. Of the eight total multiple burials, seven contain a subadult buried with an adult and one burial feature contains two adults of the opposite sex (one male, one female). In the following chapter I combine the mortuary data for these two periods of excavation.

The Trigg site yielded 283 burial features containing 313 individuals (Buchanan 1984:286–314). I have excluded one burial (Burial 301) from this count and from the following discussion because the feature appears to be intrusive to the village based on the presence of a mandrel-wound glass bead that can be dated to the eighteenth century (Brain 1979; Good 1972; Harris and Harris 1967; Stone 1974). Ubelaker, who studied the human remains from the 1971–74 Crab Orchard excavations, also supervised the analysis of the human skeletal materials from the Trigg site (Buchanan 1984:263). Multiple burials are more than twice as common at the Trigg site (11 percent) compared to the Crab Orchard site (4 percent). At the Trigg site, 15 burial features contain the remains of two individuals, 12 burials contain three individuals, and one burial contains four individuals. Most multiple burials combine an adult and a subadult within a single grave, with the subadult generally being in the infant age range (less than two years old). Several burials contain multiple subadults and, in a few instances, multiple adults are buried together. Burials with multiple adults always contain two individuals of the opposite sex.

To gain a better understanding of general mortuary practices during the Late Woodland and Protohistoric periods, I compare the two burial populations from five perspectives: age and sex composition, grave type, body position, head direction, and the proportion of individuals buried with associated nonperishable goods. The information that I present in this section has been drawn from the descriptions of burial features, human remains, and associated grave contents found in Buchanan (1984:80–108), Egloff and Reed (1980:142–145), and MacCord and Buchanan (1980:286–314). I used these descriptions to code the burial information and to create a computerized database from which I could query and tabulate the mortuary data.

Demographics of the Burial Populations

To compare the demographic composition of the two burial populations, I divide individuals into six age groups with adults further separated into male and female categories, generally following Eastman (2001). Subadults are divided into three age groups: infants (2 years and younger), children (2–5 years), and adolescents (6–15 years). Adults are grouped by sex and then further divided by age into three categories: young adults (16–25 years), mature adults (26–34 years), and older adults (35 years and older). These categories are based on physiological developments and gender-based social classes believed to represent important stages in past Native American life cycles among southern Middle Atlantic and Southeastern groups (Eastman 2001: 58–59).

At the Crab Orchard site, subadults younger than five years of age (i.e., infants and children), adult males, and adult females are represented in fairly equal frequencies, with each group comprising approximately one-quarter of the burial population (Table 5.1). Adolescents and adults of indeterminate sex each account for about one-tenth of the Crab Orchard interments. Of the 19 adults of indeterminate sex, one-half are young adults between 16 and 20 years old. The remaining individuals are recorded only as adult. At the Trigg site, subadults comprise more than one-half (56 percent) of the burial population, while adult males and adult females total approximately two-fifths (or 21 percent each) of all individuals. Infants outnumber all other age groups at

31 percent of the burial population at the Trigg site and subadults, in general, exhibit a higher mortality rate at the Trigg site (56 percent) compared to the Crab Orchard site (34 percent).

Age distributions at the Protohistoric Trigg site display a higher infant mortality (31 percent) followed by a decline in death rates during childhood (10 percent) and the adolescent (15 percent) years. This pattern represents a fairly normal mortality curve in prehistoric populations (Buikstra 1976:22; Owsley 1992:79; Wilson 1987:114). At the Crab Orchard site, infants and children (13 percent each) are represented in equal proportions followed by a decline in death during the adolescent (8 percent) years. Subadult, specifically infant and adolescent, deaths increase by more than 20 percent between the Late Woodland and Protohistoric periods. Identifying what variables created this increase and explaining why subadults died more frequently at the Trigg site is not possible at present. It may be that field collection methods and a lack of systematic recovery during the 1971–74 excavations at the Crab Orchard site resulted in fewer subadult burials identified. Future research focused on defining regional patterns of health and disease in the southern Ridge and Valley may provide additional insights into shifting demographics among Late Woodland and Protohistoric Native American populations.

Adult and subadult interments are distributed throughout both villages. The demographic composition of the two burial populations provides no evidence that individuals associated with a specific age group or sex received distinct mortuary treatments (cf., Buikstra 1981). Spatially segregated burial areas are not discernable in the archaeological record, nor does there appear to be a preference in burial location for any age group or either sex. These data suggest that families or household units frequently buried their dead in areas adjacent to their habitations. Whatever spatial groupings may be observed at the two villages were likely based on kin relations.

Grave Attributes and Body Placement

The deceased are buried in two main types of below-ground graves: simple pit and chambered pit. Simple burial features are generally oval to circular in plan with straight or sloping sides and a flat to rounded base. Chambered burials are similar in shape to simple burial features but contain a deep central or peripheral "chamber" that held the body. Shaft-and-chamber burials, as these features are often called, first appear in the archaeological record sometime following ca. A.D. 1400 and become more common with time during the Late Woodland period (Coe 1995:264; Rodning 2001:87; Ward 1987:86). Both study sites exhibit a clear preference for simple burial features (Table 5.1). At the Crab Orchard village, simple pits account for 90 percent

Table 5.1. Summary of the General Mortuary Patterns.

	Crab Orchard	Trigg
No. of Burial Features	179	283
No. of Individuals	186	313
Age and Sex Composition	$n = 186$	$n = 313$
Infant	13% (24)	31% (96)
Child	13% (25)	10% (32)
Adolescent	08% (14)	15% (46)
Adult Male	28% (52)	21% (67)
Adult Female	27% (50)	21% (67)
Adult Indeterminate	10% (19)	02% (5)
Age/Sex Indeterminate	01% (2)	—(–)
Grave Type (subadults/adults)	$n = 180$	$n = 310$
Simple	90% (162)	87% (271)
Chamber	10% (18)	13% (39)
Body Position (adults only)	$n = 99$	$n = 123$
Flexed	73% (72)	84% (103)
Extended	10% (10)	15% (18)
Bundle/Secondary	17% (17)	02% (2)
Head Direction (subadults/adults)	$n = 122$	$n = 283$
East/Northeast/Southeast	70% (86)	76% (215)
West/Northwest/Southwest	13% (16)	11% (31)
North	07% (9)	05% (13)
South	09% (11)	08% (24)
Associated Nonperishable Goods	$n = 182$	$n = 313$
Yes	32% (59)	48% (149)
No	68% (123)	52% (164)

Note: The total count (*n*) is listed for each category because indeterminate cases altered the number for which each variable could be calculated. Within each category, percent is followed by count (in parentheses).

of the burial features. This proportion is similar at the Trigg site where 87 percent of all burial features are simple pits. Chambered graves comprise 10 percent and 13 percent of the Crab Orchard and Trigg graves, respectively. Grave forms display little elaboration at either site, although occasionally some grave accouterments are present. Elaborations include lining the grave with bark or woven fiber mats and covering the body with limestone rocks, a limestone slab, or fiber mats.

Adult burials at both sites tend to be primary burials with the body interred in a flexed position (Table 5.1). Adults are also buried in an extended position or as secondary internments. The frequency of these latter two body positions differs between the two sites. At the Crab Orchard village, extended burials account for 10 percent of adult interments, while the proportion of bundle and secondary burials is higher at 17 percent of the adult interments for which body position could be determined. At the Trigg site, 15 percent of adults are interred in an extended position and 2 percent are bundle burials. Subadult burials are most often primary interments, with equal proportions noted for flexed and extended body positions.

Bundle burials are uncommon in the southern Virginia interior, northern North Carolina interior, and eastern Tennessee regions (cf., Benthall 1969; Boyd and Boyd 1992; Eastman 2001; Rodning 2001; Schroedl and Breitburg 1986; Scott and Polhemus 1987), so their high frequency at the Crab Orchard site (17 percent) is unusual. Fifteen adult and six subadult bundle burials are present, including adult males and females in each age group, adolescents, and children. Associated nonperishable goods are typically absent (90 percent) from these graves. The bundle burials at the Trigg site similarly lack grave goods. In addition, six secondary burials in which the remains are described as scattered rather than bundled are also present.

Secondary interments represent one part of an extended mortuary ritual in which the bones of the deceased are processed before final burial (Hutchinson and Aragon 2002:47). The body may lay exposed above-ground on a burial scaffold or in a charnel structure or below-ground in a crypt or stone box grave for a prescribed period often dictated by time or the later death of an important individual. Relatives of the deceased later return to the body to collect the bones and rebury them. In total, 27 secondary interments are recorded for the Crab Orchard site. These burials exhibit a pattern identical to the primary interments in the proportion of individuals buried in simple vs. chambered grave types. Secondary burials are found throughout the village and also appear to be comparable to primary burials in their spatial distribution.

At both sites there is a preference for burying the dead with their head placed in an easterly direction. Of the interments for which head direction could be determined, 70 percent and 76 percent are buried with their head oriented toward the east at the Crab Orchard and Trigg sites, respectively (Table 5.1). An easterly orientation in burials is fairly common throughout the greater study region (Boyd and Boyd 1992:254–255; Ward 1987:86).

Mortuary treatment does not appear to differ by age group or sex. Variation in grave type and burial position is similar among subadults and adults of both sexes. Furthermore, there is neither archaeological nor ethnohistoric evidence that suggests that individuals in any of these groups received alternative modes of burial treatment such as interment in a charnel house or earthen mound.

Associated Nonperishable Goods

The most marked difference in burial practices between the two sites is the proportion of individuals buried with associated nonperishable goods. These objects can be divided into two categories based on the source of the material used to manufacture the item: (1) those that could be acquired from materials available locally, and (2) those produced from nonlocal materials acquired through interregional trade or gift-exchanges. Mortuary items manufactured from local materials include bone beads and pendants, animal teeth and claws, turtle carapace cups, ceramic pots, pipes, bone and stone tools, and toolkits. The primary nonlocal items obtained by southern Ridge and Valley residents are marine shell, copper, and, during the Protohistoric period, copper-alloy ornaments, glass beads, and the occasional iron object. In the remaining chapter, I use the word "copper" to refer to both copper and copper-alloy metals. Distinguishing between the two often requires an analysis of the chemical composition of the artifact. Copper mined from North American sources test high in purity levels, while European copper-alloys recovered from southern Ridge and Valley archaeological sites exhibit several different chemical signatures that vary in the proportion of zinc, lead, and antimony (M. B. Barber, Solberg, and Barfield 1996).

At both the Crab Orchard and Trigg sites, infants and children are buried with similar types of nonperishable goods (Figures 5.1 and 5.2). These items include ceramics pots, turtle carapace cups, carnivore teeth and claws (generally bear, mountain lion, bobcat, or wolf), raptor talons (usually eagle or hawk), and marine shell and copper ornaments. With the exception of a single stone bead, locally produced goods are absent in adolescent graves at the Crab Orchard village, and they occur only slightly more often in child and infant burials during the Late Woodland period. At the Protohistoric Trigg site, adolescents generally receive similar goods as infants and children

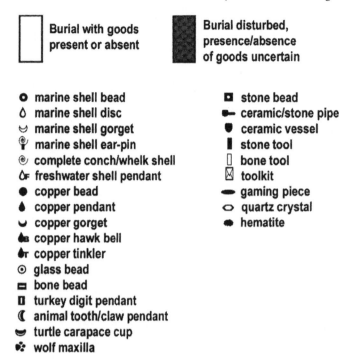

Figure 5.1. Key of symbols used to illustrate the distribution of nonperishable mortuary goods in Figures 5.2, 5.3, and 5.4.

with a few new types of goods entering into the suite such as turkey wing digit pendants and stone tools. Overall, there are more subadults being buried with a wider assortment of goods during the Protohistoric period.

Adult women received some similar types of goods upon burial during the Late Woodland and Protohistoric periods. These mortuary items include shell beads and pendants, ceramic vessels, animal bone beads and pendants, and the occasional stone tool. At the Protohistoric Trigg site, women were also buried with turtle carapace cups, toolkits, a gaming piece, and one burial contained copper beads (Figures 5.1 and 5.3). Adult men show a dramatic shift in mortuary goods, both in terms of the types of goods and the quantity of goods, between the Late Woodland and Protohistoric periods. The most well-provisioned male burials during the Late Woodland period belong to older men. Older men received smoking pipes, animal teeth pendants, copper, marine shell, carnivore bone tools, and toolkits more often than mature and younger men. During the Protohistoric period, the most well provisioned burials belong mostly to young men. More younger men are buried with marine shell, copper, and toolkits compared to mature and older men (Fig-

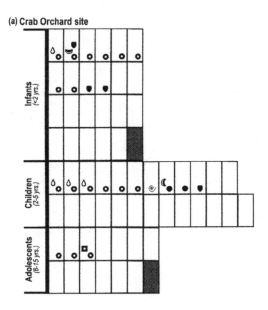

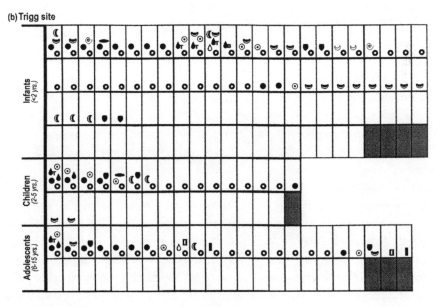

Figure 5.2 a and b. Distribution of nonperishable mortuary goods by burial for subadults, (a) Crab Orchard site, (b) Trigg site.

ures 5.1 and 5.4). Young men are also interred with smoking pipes, carnivore teeth and claw pendants, carnivore bone tools, and ceramic vessels. During the Protohistoric period, several of the young male burials at the Trigg site take on the appearance of the most elaborate older male burials at the Late Woodland Crab Orchard site.

Several categories of nonperishable locally produced mortuary goods require further comment. The distribution of ceramic vessels, for example, broadens during the Protohistoric period. At the Crab Orchard site, vessels are buried with infants, children, older women, and mature and older men, whereas at the Trigg site this list expands to include adolescents as well as young men and women. A recent analysis of complete and reconstructed ceramic vessels from select contexts at the Trigg site determined that vessels from burial contexts have a median diameter below that of vessels recovered from feature contexts (Klein, Martin, and Duncan 2003). Vessels interred with the deceased also exhibit burnished and plain surface treatments more often than ceramics produced for utilitarian use. Michael Klein and colleagues suggest that, rather than interring utilitarian vessels with the dead, certain vessels were produced specifically to be used as grave goods. Turtle carapace cups, which are found in one infant grave at the Crab Orchard village, also show a broader distribution at the Trigg site where they are found with subadults, adult females, and older adult males (Figures 5.1, 5.2, 5.3, and 5.4). When turkey wing digit pendants (*Meleagris gallapavo* wing digit II, phalanx I) are found with adult burials, they are associated only with young females at both of the sites.

Several categories of local mortuary items are restricted among the adult population to adult males. Male items at both sites include carnivore teeth and claws, raptor talons, pipes, and bone and stone tools, however there are exceptions to this latter category. At the Crab Orchard site, one young female (Burial 21) is buried with two stone celts along with 75 olive shell beads, 258 turkey wing digit pendants, three tubular bone beads, and a marine shell ear pin. At the Trigg site, two mature females are buried with stone tools contained within a toolkit. The toolkit of one mature female (Burial 53) contains three stone scrapers, three triangular projectile points, and five utilized flakes. The second mature female (Burial 273) is buried with a toolkit that contains one stone celt, nine projectile points, flaking tools, a shell scraper, a beaver tooth, a turtle shell cup, a worked mammal femur, and a lump of clay.

The broader distribution and increased frequency of toolkits at the Protohistoric Trigg site is notable. Only two toolkits are found at the Late Woodland Crab Orchard site, both with older adult males (Burials 24 and 68). At the Trigg site, a total of eight toolkits are present in burials, four with young

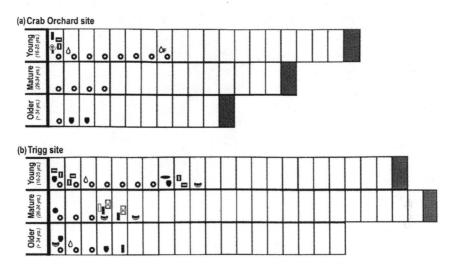

Figure 5.3. Distribution of nonperishable mortuary goods by burial for adult females, (a) Crab Orchard site, (b) Trigg site.

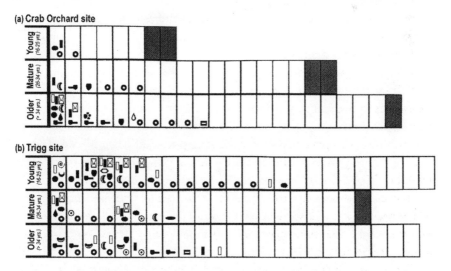

Figure 5.4. Distribution of nonperishable mortuary goods by burial for adult males, (a) Crab Orchard site, (b) Trigg site.

3 in.
8 cm.

Figure 5.5. Sand-tempered ceramic effigy vessel recovered from a young adult male burial (Burial 34) at the Trigg site. Image reproduced with permission of the Virginia Department of Historic Resources.

males (Burials 34, 68, 246, and 303), two with mature males (Burials 247 and 252), and two with mature females (Burials 53 and 273). The location of tool-kits within graves is not consistently noted in the Trigg site report; however, when this information was available these items were found in the head, shoulder, or upper arm region. Interestingly, the only beamer, a bone hide-working tool, found in a mortuary context is contained within a toolkit buried with a young male (Burial 34) 20–25 years old at the Protohistoric Trigg site. In addition to the deer metatarsal beamer, the toolkit also contains two chert knives, two spokeshaves, one projectile point, various utilized flakes and lithic debitage and three antler flaking tools. Other grave goods include a mountain lion claw (*Puma concolor* 3rd phalanx), a quartz crystal, and an unusual ceramic vessel with molded turtle and snake figurines (Figure 5.5).

In terms of the distribution of nonperishable grave goods by age and sex category, about one-third (32 percent) of the Crab Orchard burial population is interred with some type of good. This frequency increases at the Trigg site where almost half (48 percent) of all deceased individuals are buried with associated goods (see Table 5.1). Although more individuals receive non-perishable goods upon burial during the Protohistoric period, these goods are not evenly distributed across the burial population. Of the subadult popula-

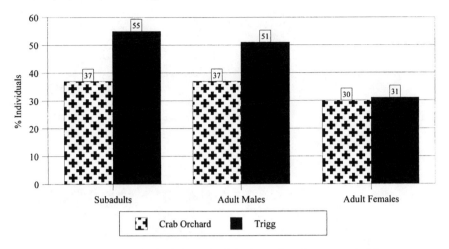

Figure 5.6. Proportion of subadults and adults buried with nonperishable mortuary goods.

tion, 37 percent of subadults are buried with nonperishable goods at the Crab Orchard site. This proportion increases at the Trigg site where more than one-half (55 percent) of the subadult population received goods upon burial (Figure 5.6 and Table 5.2). Similarly, at the Crab Orchard site, 37 percent of adult males of all adult males are buried with grave goods. This proportion increases again at the Trigg site to 51 percent, just over one-half of all adult males are buried with some type of nonperishable good during the Protohistoric period. The data on adult females do not follow the same pattern. At the Crab Orchard site, 30 percent of adult females of the total adult female population are buried with grave goods. This frequency is almost identical at the Trigg site where 31 percent of the adult female population received nonperishable goods upon burial.

Considering the distribution of mortuary items within the adult population provides further insights into who is, and who is not, being buried with nonperishable goods. Age categories follow those outlined in the previous section: young (16–25 years), mature (26–34 years), and older (35 years and older). The trend for women is almost identical between the Crab Orchard and Trigg sites. Between 40 and 43 percent of young females of all young females are buried with some type of nonperishable good, while mature and older females received goods about 25 percent of the time compared to their respective burial populations (Figure 5.7a and Table 5.2). As women grow older they are less likely to be buried with grave goods. The pattern differs among men at the two sites. At the Crab Orchard site the proportion of men

(a)

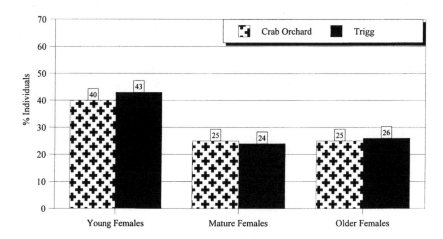

(b)

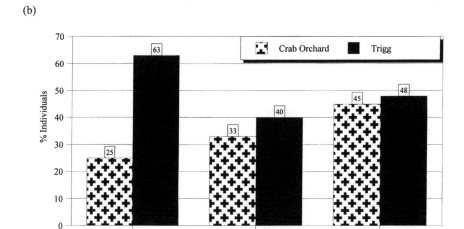

Figure 5.7. Proportion of (a) adult females and (b) adult males buried with nonperishable mortuary goods.

buried with nonperishable goods increases with age: 25 percent of young males of all young males received grave goods, 33 percent of mature males, and 45 percent of older males. During the Late Woodland period, as men grow older they are more likely to be buried with goods. This trend changes dramatically during the Protohistoric period, however. Of their respective burial populations, 63 percent of young males, 40 percent of mature males, and 48 percent of older males at the Trigg site received nonperishable goods

Table 5.2. Frequency of Nonperishable Mortuary Goods by Age and Sex.

	Crab Orchard	Trigg
Subadults with Goods	37% (23)	55% (94)
of All Subadults	$n = 63$	$n = 174$
Adult Males with Goods	37% (19)	51% (34)
of All Adult Males	$n = 52$	$n = 67$
Adult Females with Goods	30% (15)	31% (21)
of All Adult Females	$n = 50$	$n = 67$
Young Females with Goods	40% (8)	43% (10)
of All Young Females	$n = 20$	$n = 23$
Mature Females with Goods	25% (4)	24% (6)
of All Mature Females	$n = 16$	$n = 25$
Older Females with Goods	25% (3)	26% (5)
of All Older Females	$n = 12$	$n = 19$
Young Males with Goods	25% (2)	63% (15)
of All Young Males	$n = 8$	$n = 24$
Mature Males with Goods	33% (6)	40% (8)
of All Mature Males	$n = 18$	$n = 20$
Older Males with Goods	45% (10)	48% (11)
of All Older Males	$n = 22$	$n = 23$

Note: Count follows percent; total count (*n*) listed below. The Crab Orchard site also contains one individual of unknown age and sex and one adult male of unknown age buried with local goods.

upon burial (Figure 5.7b and Table 5.2). The proportion of older males buried with goods is almost identical between the Crab Orchard and Trigg sites, while slightly more mature males received goods upon burial during the Protohistoric period. The most striking difference between the two sites is the proportion of young males buried with nonperishable goods. Young men are more than twice as likely to be buried with goods during Protohistoric period compared to the Late Woodland period.

Summary

General mortuary practices at the Crab Orchard and Trigg sites exhibit many similar traits, especially in grave form and body placement. About three-quarters of all individuals at both sites are buried in a flexed position in a simple pit with the head placed in an easterly direction. Interments are typically primary burials located near domestic structures, although variations such as multiple burials and secondary interments occur. Spatial groupings seem to be based on family or kin units, not age or sex or social class. These similarities end, however, when the final variable is considered. Many more individuals (16 percent more) are buried with nonperishable grave goods during the Protohistoric period. These objects are not evenly distributed throughout the burial population, however. Children, adolescents, and men are buried with nonperishable goods in disproportionate numbers compared to women during the Protohistoric period. In particular, the proportion of young men who received goods upon burial increases significantly. To explore these patterns more fully I turn now to examine the mortuary contexts of nonlocal goods, items that could only have been obtained through interregional trade or gift-exchanges.

Nonlocal Goods in Mortuary Contexts

During the Late Woodland period, two nonlocal materials, marine shell and copper, were the primary items obtained by southern Ridge and Valley residents through interregional exchanges. This list expands in the Protohistoric period to include European-manufactured items which were generally limited to copper-alloy ornaments and glass beads during the time period considered. The information presented in this section combines data from both periods of excavation at the Crab Orchard site as presented in MacCord and Buchanan (1980:80–108, 118) and Egloff and Reed (1980:136–138, 142–145) and as found in the Virginia Department of Historic Resources specimen catalog. The Trigg site data is based on artifact counts by Patricia Sternheimer (1983:73, 105) combined with more general information found in Buchanan (1984:286–314). The descriptions of the glass bead assemblage from the Trigg site are from my own analysis.

Marine Shell

Approximately 6,500 marine shell artifacts were recovered from 41 burials at the Crab Orchard site. Beads are the most common shell artifact form with several bead types and shell species represented, including columella (*Buscy-*

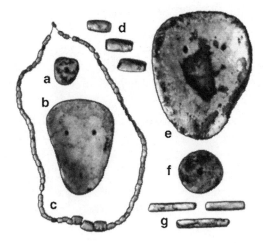

Figure 5.8. Marine shell artifacts from the Trigg site, (a) shell disk, (b) *Busycon* spp. shell gorget, (c) barrel-shaped *Busycon* spp. shell beads, (d) Olividae beads, (e) *Busycon* spp. shell gorget, (f) shell disk, (g) *Busycon* spp. columnella beads. Image reproduced with permission of the Virginia Department of Historic Resources.

con spp.), marginella (*Prunum* spp.), and olive (*Oliva* spp. and *Olivella* spp.) beads and disk-shaped beads manufactured from an indeterminate marine shell source (Figure 5.8). More than two-thirds of the individuals interred with shell beads at the Crab Orchard site are buried with either columella or olive beads and slightly more than one-quarter are buried with marginella beads. Small disk-shaped beads, although present in the Crab Orchard mortuary assemblage, are found with only two individuals. In addition to beads, columella pendants are present in four subadult graves (Burials 8, 36, 77, and 138) and two adult graves (Burials 98 and 144), and one child burial (Burial 2) contains a complete immature conch shell.

The Trigg site yielded more than 21,800 marine shell artifacts from 104 burials. Shell species and bead types are similar to those identified at the Crab Orchard site. Pendants are present in two subadult graves (Burials 6 and 32) and two adult female interments (Burials 49 and 206). Two infant burials (Burials 151 and 205) contain marine shell gorgets. In addition, complete conch or whelk shells are present in two infant burials (Burials 140 and 200) and one young male burial (Burial 194). Small disk-shaped beads are interred with more individuals (38 percent) than any other bead form. This contrasts to the low frequency of these beads at the Crab Orchard site. Disk-shaped beads, which are common in seventeenth-century marine shell assemblages from southern Virginia and northern North Carolina, were likely produced from the wall sections of large univalve shells (Hammett and Sizemore 1989: 130). Of the individuals buried with shell beads at the Trigg site, 30 percent received columella beads and 26 percent marginella beads. Less than one-tenth (7 percent) of the burial population that received shell beads upon burial are interred with olive beads.

Shifts in marine shell bead distributions between the two sites suggest that several changes took place in the use of shell beads between the Late Wood-land and Protohistoric periods. Olive beads decline in frequency, falling out of use altogether by the mid-seventeenth century in the Virginia and North Carolina interior. The use of small disk-shaped beads increases dramatically during the Protohistoric period. In the North Carolina piedmont, these beads tend to be the predominant form in seventeenth-century marine shell assem-blages (Hammett 1987; Hammett and Sizemore 1989). A more detailed study of the marine shell artifacts from the study sites is needed in order to deter-mine whether the observed changes resulted from shifts in bead manufacture, resource accessibility, directionality of exchange systems, or a combination of these and other factors.

Marine shell ornaments, except for shell gorgets, crosscut all age and sex categories. Shell beads and pendants are found with infants, children, adoles-cents, and adults at both sites (see Figures 5.1, 5.2, 5.3, and 5.4). Shell gorgets are uncommon, with only two of these items found in infant burials (Burial 151 and 205) at the Trigg site. The proportion of individuals buried with ma-rine shell is almost identical between the Crab Orchard and Trigg sites. Of all individuals buried with some type of nonperishable good, 69 percent are buried with marine shell at the Late Woodland Crab Orchard site and 70 percent received marine shell upon burial at the Protohistoric Trigg site (Table 5.3).

The distribution of marine shell artifacts between the two sites is not simi-lar in every way, however. The maximum, median, and average number of marine shell artifacts per individual buried with marine shell increases during the Protohistoric period. The minimum number, which is always one, re-mains the same. The maximum number of marine shell objects in any one grave rises 600 count, from ca. 2,300 at the Crab Orchard site to ca. 2,900 at the Trigg site (Table 5.3). These numbers are best estimates because some-times shell count was recorded as an approximate number in the site reports. The median marine shell count more than doubles between the Late Wood-land and Protohistoric periods, from 24 at the Crab Orchard site to 65 at the Trigg site, and the average number of marine shell items per individual buried

Table 5.3. Summary Statistics for the Nonlocal Mortuary Goods.

	Crab Orchard	Trigg
Marine Shell		
Total Count	ca. 6,500+	ca. 21,800+
No. of Individuals Buried with Shell	41	104
% Buried with Shell	69%	70%
No. of Shell Items per Burial		
Minimum	1	1
Maximum	2,300	2,900
Median	24	65
Average	161	255
Copper		
Total Count	25	ca. 250
No. of Individuals Buried with Copper	3	31
% Buried with Copper	5%	21%
No. of Copper Items per Burial		
Minimum	1	1
Maximum	13	148
Median	11	4
Average	8	18
Glass Beads		
Total Count		348
No. of Individuals Buried with Glass Beads		16
% Buried with Glass Beads		11%
No. of Glass Beads per Burial		
Minimum		1
Maximum		195
Median		6
Average		22

with marine shell also increases, from 161 at the Crab Orchard site to 255 at the Trigg site.

In sum, both the Late Woodland and Protohistoric periods display similar proportions of individuals in the burial population interred with marine shell, however the dead are buried with much larger quantities of this material during the Protohistoric period.

Copper

Copper, like marine shell, is also present at both sites. Three Crab Orchard site burials contain a total of 25 copper ornaments. Two of these burials are located approximately 27 m from each other in the east-central portion of the village. One child burial (Burial 28) contains 11 tubular copper beads found near the cranium. The beads measure 18 mm in length by 2 mm in diameter (MacCord and Buchanan 1980:85). No other grave goods are present. Another child burial (Burial 507A9) yields one copper bead and several olivella beads that encircled the neck (Egloff and Reed 1980:138). This grave is located inside a domestic structure in the northwest portion of the village (see Figure 2.3). In addition, numerous black bear foot bones surrounded the body, which initially suggested that the child may have been wrapped in bear skins upon burial (Egloff and Reed 1980:141). A detailed analysis of the associated bear bones in the present study identified 252 elements from the fore- and hind-feet of at least 10 different animals. These bones are generally complete elements with no burning noted and few scarred by butchery (only four of the 252 bones exhibit cut marks). The black bear bones associated with Burial 507A9 were excluded from the Chapter 3 summary of the general Crab Orchard fauna.

An older male burial (Burial 68) at the Crab Orchard site yields 12 tubular copper beads and a triangular-shaped piece of copper, identified only as a "fragment," from the neck region (MacCord and Buchanan 1980:90–91). The beads measure on average 55 mm in length by 5 mm in diameter. This burial also contains a toolkit found to the northeast of the cranium that includes: a knife, two projectile points, utilized flakes and cores, two hematite fragments, a smoking pipe, two bone needles and two awls, a flaking tool manufactured from a black bear baculum, four bobcat hindlimb bones, and two viperidae snake fangs (MacCord and Buchanan 1980:90–91).

The Trigg site yields approximately 520 copper artifacts from 31 burials, represented by 14 infants (Burials 59, 79, 94, 109, 127, 136, 159, 161, 197, 200, 205, 227, 242, and 245), five children (Burials 22, 75, 155, 238, and 272), eight adolescents (Burials 21, 23, 244, 274, 279, 292, 296, and 297), two young males (Burials 194 and 233), one mature/older male (Burial 247), and one mature female (Burial 291). Figure 5.9 shows some of these ornaments. Artifact forms include several sizes of rolled tubular beads, triangular- and circular-shaped pendants, a fishhook- or claw-shaped effigy pendant, a large circular gorget, numerous rolled tinklers, which Buchanan described as both bangles and cones, and a small bell known as a "hawk bell." Beads are by far the most common artifact form. Twenty-five burials contain rolled tubular beads with sizes ranging from 3 mm to 84 mm in length and 2 mm to 12 mm in diameter (Buchanan 1984:322). Bead placement on the body indicates that the Trigg site residents wore these items most often as necklaces and sometimes as bracelets and earrings. Beads were occasionally sewn into garments, attached to leather bags, and woven into hair. Copper pendants are present in three subadult graves (Burials 22, 23, 75) and one mature male interment (Burial 247) and five subadult burials (Burials 23, 75, 109, 205, and 227) contain rolled tinklers. Half of a hawk bell was found in an infant burial (Burial 127). The most impressive copper artifact recovered from the Trigg site is a large gorget found with a young male (Burial 194) (Figure 5.10). This item measures 124 mm by 131 mm in diameter (Buchanan 1984:322). Researchers have suggested that the gorget may be Spanish in origin, possibly associated with the A.D. 1540s expedition by de Soto (MacCord 1989b:125) or, more likely, the post-1580s Spanish explorations and trade (Waselkov 1989:123).

Unlike marine shell, the distribution of copper artifacts differs in all regards between the two sites. At the Crab Orchard site, two children and an older male are buried with copper. This pattern shifts at the Trigg site where copper items are most frequently buried with adolescents followed closely by children and infants. Young males are buried with copper in two instances. One mature/older male and one mature female also received copper items upon burial. The number of individuals buried with copper increases fourfold during the Protohistoric period. Of individuals buried with nonperishable goods of any kind, only 5 percent are buried with copper at the Crab Orchard site, while more than one-fifth (21 percent) received copper upon burial at the Trigg site (see Table 5.3). Furthermore, the raw count of copper artifacts is more than 20 times greater at the Trigg site ($n = 520$) compared to the Crab Orchard site ($n = 25$). The maximum, median, and average number of copper artifacts per individual buried with this material type also differs between the two sites. The maximum number of copper objects in any one grave increases from 13 at the Crab Orchard site to 148 at the Trigg site. The average number of copper objects doubles, from eight at the Crab Orchard site to 18 at the Trigg site. The median decreases, however, from 11 at the Crab Orchard site to four at the Trigg site.

Copper artifacts are few in number and restricted in distribution to a few

Figure 5.9. Copper artifacts from the Trigg site, (a) tinklers, (b) large rolled beads, (c) small rolled beads, (d) fishhook/claw effigy pendant, (e–f) triangular-shaped pendants.

Figure 5.10. Copper gorget from the Trigg site. Image reproduced with permission of the Virginia Department of Historic Resources.

burials during the Late Woodland period. Although the Crab Orchard site predates permanent English settlement in Virginia, for most of the previous century Spanish explorers had traveled, traded, and plundered throughout the interior Southeast. These sixteenth-century Spanish expeditions commanded by Hernando de Soto, Tristan de Luna, Juan Pardo, and others introduced southeastern Native Americans to a variety of European goods (Clayton, Knight, and Moore 1993; Hudson 1990). There is a slight chance that some of the copper artifacts at the Crab Orchard site may be from a European source, although the copper tested to date is North American in origin (Egloff 1992:205).

In contrast, during the Protohistoric period, both the number of copper artifacts and the proportion of individuals buried with copper increases significantly. These changes suggest to me that the copper entering southern Ridge and Valley exchange networks during the seventeenth century was not North American in origin, but rather the product of a new, European source of copper (i.e., copper-alloy). Without conducting chemical composition tests on the copper from the Trigg site it is impossible to know for certain whether all of the copper is European in origin. Certain items, however, such as the hawk bell, are undoubtedly of European manufacture. Copper tinklers, which are found in three subadult burials at the Trigg site, are an artifact form believed to have been produced from European sheet metal (e.g., Bradley 1977:11; Kent 1984:203–204; Kraft 1972:52; Mayer-Oakes 1955: 122; Smith 1987:37; Wall and Lapham 2003:166–167; Wells 2002:99) and the large copper gorget interred with a young male has been linked to Spanish explorations in the late sixteenth- and early seventeenth-century Southeast (MacCord 1989b:125; Waselkov 1989:123).

Glass Beads

Glass beads first enter Native American exchange networks with the arrival of European explorers and settlers during the sixteenth and seventeenth centuries. Although the Crab Orchard site dates to a time when the Spanish were exploring interior regions to the south, terminal Late Woodland southern Ridge and Valley residents likely had no contact with these foreigners nor with the goods they brought to trade. European items have not been identified at the Crab Orchard site, but the possibility exists that future archaeological excavations may yield European artifacts or further testing of the existing copper artifacts may find them to be from a non-North American source. At present, however, glass beads are found only at the Protohistoric Trigg site, which precludes a comparison of these artifacts between the two sites. In the following section glass is compared to copper in order to gauge the relative frequency of these two materials in the Protohistoric period.

There have been three prior analyses of the glass beads from the Trigg site, one by MacCord (1977:60–63), another by Sternheimer (1983:71), and a third by Buchanan (1984:323–324). Each study differs from the other in the types of beads identified and the frequency of each variety. Rather than prioritize one analysis over another I chose to reexamine the glass bead assemblage. In doing so I retyped the beads following the Kidd and Kidd (1970) classification system. Table 5.4 provides a description and count of each variety. Figure 5.11 pictures some of the beads. My analysis is briefly summarized below.

The glass bead collection from the Trigg site consists largely of three varieties of white-colored beads (IIa13, IIa15, and IVa11). Small, circular, cored white beads (IVa11) comprise approximately two-thirds (65 percent) of the assemblage, while about one-fifth (22 percent) are round and oval uncored white beads (IIa13, IIa15). The fourth most common bead variety, which comprises only 5 percent of the collection, is a round robins-egg blue bead decorated with white stripes (IIb56/57). Undecorated round robins-egg blue beads (IIa40) and small, circular red-striped white beads (IVb13*) are also present. Most beads are undecorated (94 percent), with cored varieties (68 percent) more common than uncored beads (32 percent).

A total of 348 glass beads are present in 16 burials, representing five infants (Burials 109, 154, 157, 181, and 227), four children (Burials 22, 75, 84, and 238), three adolescents (Burials 18, 23, and 111), two mature males (Burials 39 and 88), and two older males (Burials 236 and 271). Glass beads are found most frequently with subadults. Subadults, primarily infants and children, account for 75 percent (n = 12) of the individuals buried with glass and contain 93 percent (n = 325) of the total number of glass beads. Glass beads are absent in young male and adult female burials.

Compared to the number of copper artifacts (n = 520) and proportion of individuals buried with copper (n = 31), glass beads are found in lower quantities (n = 348) and are buried with fewer individuals (n = 16). Of individuals buried with nonperishable goods of any kind, 21 percent are buried with copper and 11 percent with glass (see Table 5.3). Although glass beads are buried with fewer individuals, when present they are found in slightly greater quantities than copper. The maximum, median, and average number of glass beads (195, 6, 22) per burial is higher than the figures for copper (148, 4, 18).

Distribution of Nonlocal Goods

The distribution of nonlocal goods in mortuary contexts differs by material type. Marine shell ornaments, with the exception of shell gorgets, crosscut all

6 cm.

Figure 5.11. Glass beads from the Trigg site, (a) IVk4, IVb13*, IIa40, IIa13,
(b) IIa55, IIa_*1, (c) IIa_*1, IIa_*2, IIa40, (d) IVa11, (e) IIa40, IIb56/57, IVk4,
(f) IIa13, IIa15, IIa40.

age and sex categories. Copper, in contrast, is restricted to children and older
men during the Late Woodland period. Dispersal of copper broadens during
the Protohistoric period to include infants, children, adolescents, young men,
a mature/older man, and a mature woman. Glass beads are slightly more
restricted than copper during the Protohistoric period in that they occur with
infants, children, adolescents, mature men, and older men. Neither young
men nor women of any age were buried with glass beads. These data, combined with information on the quantity of nonlocal materials, suggest that a
shift occurred during the Protohistoric period toward more people being
buried with nonlocal goods and toward people being buried with greater
quantities of these items. Such changes may be related to a changing ideology
that placed greater value or emphasis on the expression of social differences
in material forms. This hypothesis leads to another important question—
who, precisely, is getting these goods?

Marine shell is the only nonlocal material found in large enough quantities
during both the Late Woodland and Protohistoric periods to allow for the
data to be graphed in a meaningful way, so the following comparisons focus

Table 5.4. Glass Beads from Mortuary Contexts at the Trigg Site.

Kidd Variety (n = 348)		Description
IIa_*1	(3)	Small to large, round, translucent dark blue-green beads; Munsell 2.5BG 4/6–4/8
IIa_*2	(1)	Medium, round, translucent dark aqua blue bead; Munsell 10BG 3/8
IIa13	(37)	Medium to large, round, opaque white beads; Munsell GY-G 9/5GY
IIa15	(41)	Medium, oval, opaque white beads; Munsell GY-G 9/10GY
IIa40	(5)	Medium to large, round, opaque robins egg blue beads; Munsell varies (5B 4/6, 2.5B 4/6–5/6, 10B 4/6)
IIa40?	(4)	Possibly medium, round, opaque robins egg blue beads; Beads on loan
IIa41	(1)	Small, circular, opaque robins egg blue bead; Munsell indeterminate (bead too deteriorated)
IIa46	(1)	Small, round, opaque shadow blue bead; Munsell 5PB 4/6
IIa55	(1)	Medium, round, translucent navy blue bead; Munsell 5PB 2/8
IIb56/57	(18)	Large, round, opaque robins egg blue beads with three or four white stripes; Munsell varies (5B 4/6, 2.5B 4/6–5/6)
IVa_*	(2)	Small, circular, translucent bright blue beads with two glass layers (tl. bright blue/tp. bright blue); Munsell 10BG 5/6
IVa11	(227)	Small, circular, white beads with three glass layers (tp. colorless/op. white /tp. colorless); Munsell GY-G 9/5GY
IVa16*	(1)	Large, round, navy blue bead with three glass layers (tl. navy blue/op. white/tl. navy blue); Bead on loan

IVb13* (4) Small, circular, white beads with 6 red stripes and comprised of three glass layers (tp. colorless/op. white/tp. colorless); Munsell GY-G 9/5GY (white), 7.5R 3/10 (red)

IVk4 (2) Medium to large, round, navy blue beads comprised of five glass layers (tl. navy blue/op. white/op. redwood/ op. white/ tl. navy blue); Munsell 5PB 2/8 (exterior layer)

Note: Four "medium blue" beads, most likely representing the IIa40 variety, are on loan to the Glencoe Museum in Radford, Virginia, and could not be positively identified. This table excludes one glass bead recovered from an intrusive burial and two beads found in feature contexts. Beads that exhibit two or more glass layers have the glass diaphanity and color of each layer listed in parentheses, beginning with the exterior layer and ending with the central core. Abbreviations used include transparent (tp.), translucent (tl.), and opaque (op.).

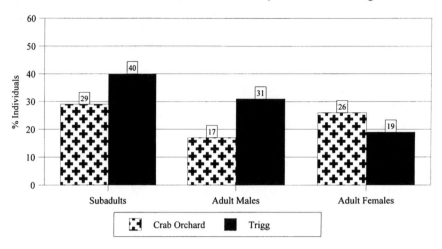

Figure 5.12. Proportion of subadults and adults buried with marine shell.

solely on this material type. Of the subadult population, persons 15 years of age and younger, 29 percent are buried with marine shell at the Crab Orchard site and 40 percent received shell upon burial at the Trigg site (Figure 5.12 and Table 5.5). Among adult males, 17 percent are buried with marine shell at the Crab Orchard site. This figure increases to 31 percent at the Trigg site. The trend reverses for women. Of the adult female population, 26 percent received marine shell upon burial at the Crab Orchard site and 19 percent are buried with shell at the Trigg site. During the Late Woodland period, subadults and women are more likely to be buried with marine shell, while subadults and men are most likely to be interred with shell during the Protohistoric period. Moreover, at the Protohistoric Trigg site, the average number of marine shell objects per burial is significantly higher for subadults (225) and men (232) than it is for women (45).

Considering the distribution of marine shell within the adult population provides further insights into who was, and who was not, being buried with goods obtained through interregional exchanges. Age categories follow those outlined above: young (16–25 years), mature (26–34 years), and older (35 years and older). At the Crab Orchard site the proportion of women buried with marine shell decreases with age: 40 percent of young females receive shell upon burial, 25 percent of mature females, and 8 percent of older females (Figure 5.13a). During the Late Woodland period, as women grow older they are less likely to be buried with marine shell. The pattern for women is generally similar at the Trigg site where 30 percent of young females, 12 percent of mature females, and 16 percent of older females are buried with ma-

Table 5.5. Frequency of Marine Shell Mortuary Goods by Age and Sex.

	Crab Orchard	Trigg
Subadults with Shell	29% (18)	40% (70)
of All Subadults	$n = 63$	$n = 174$
Adult Males with Shell	17% (9)	31% (21)
of All Adult Males	$n = 52$	$n = 67$
Adult Females with Shell	26% (13)	19% (13)
of All Adult Females	$n = 50$	$n = 67$
Young Females with Shell	40% (8)	30% (7)
of All Young Females	$n = 20$	$n = 23$
Mature Females with Shell	25% (4)	12% (3)
of All Mature Females	$n = 16$	$n = 25$
Older Females with Shell	08% (1)	16% (3)
of All Older Females	$n = 12$	$n = 19$
Young Males with Shell	25% (2)	54% (13)
of All Young Males	$n = 8$	$n = 24$
Mature Males with Shell	17% (3)	20% (4)
of All Mature Males	$n = 18$	$n = 20$
Older Males with Shell	18% (4)	17% (4)
of All Older Males	$n = 22$	$n = 23$

Note: Count follows percent; total count (n) listed below.

rine shell. During the Protohistoric period, older women received marine shell slightly more often than mature women. When these distributions are compared between the two sites it is apparent that the proportion of women buried with marine shell declines during the Protohistoric period, with the exception of older women who are twice as likely to be buried with shell in this latter period.

Men, in contrast, exhibit two very different patterns. At the Late Woodland Crab Orchard site, marine shell is buried with just a slightly higher proportion of young males (25 percent) compare to mature and older males

(a)

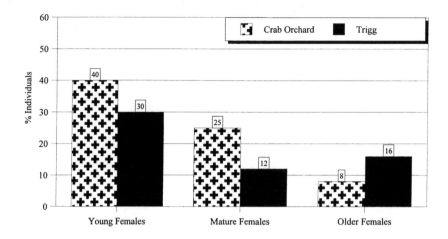

(b)

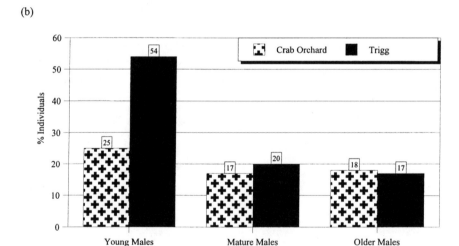

Figure 5.13. Proportion of (a) adult females and (b) adult males buried with marine shell.

(17 percent and 18 percent, respectively), while the Protohistoric Trigg site shows a marked increase in the proportion of young males who received marine shell upon burial (Figure 5.13b). Of their respective burial populations, 54 percent of young males, 20 percent of mature males, and 17 percent of older males are buried with marine shell at the Trigg site. When the two patterns are compared to each other it is evident that mature and older males receive marine shell in similar frequencies during both the Late Woodland

and Protohistoric periods. The most striking difference between these two burial populations is the significantly greater (29 percent greater) proportion of young men buried with marine shell at the Protohistoric Trigg site.

Mortuary Practices and Prestige Goods Use in a Protohistoric Context

Changes evident in Protohistoric mortuary practices suggest that increased importance was placed on the expression of social differences in material forms, at least in funerary contexts. The Trigg site occupants buried their dead with greater quantities of nonperishable goods and more people received goods upon burial than had in the past. Although more individuals are buried with nonperishable goods during the Protohistoric period, these items are not evenly distributed across the burial population. Grave goods show an asymmetrical distribution, with children, adolescents, and men associated with both local and nonlocal goods in disproportionate numbers compared to women. The overall higher frequency of nonlocal goods, in particular, represents one outcome of increased interregional exchanges associated with participation in a new and rapidly growing trade in processed deerskins. Producing surplus hides for trade gave the Trigg site residents greater access to nonlocal, socially valued materials.

Several notable differences exist within the adult burial populations between the Late Woodland and Protohistoric periods. The proportion of adult females buried with nonperishable goods is almost identical during the two periods, with more young women receiving goods upon burial than mature and older women. These patterns differ somewhat for nonlocal goods. During the Late Woodland period, the proportion of adult females buried with nonlocal goods, which are limited to marine shell ornaments, decreases with age. This trend is also evident during the Protohistoric period, except that mature and older women are buried with nonlocal goods in similarly low frequencies. During both periods, women in their prime childbearing years are almost twice as likely to be buried with marine shell compared to mature and older women. These data suggest that as women aged their status changed and its expression manifested in other, nonmaterial ways that have not survived in the mortuary record. Comparing the Late Woodland and Protohistoric female burial populations indicates that the proportion of women buried with nonlocal goods decreases from previous times during the seventeenth century. This decline may reflect changing attitudes among and toward women in the Protohistoric Trigg community. I explore these possibilities in greater detail in the following chapter.

In contrast to women, men exhibit two different patterns. During the Late Woodland period, men are buried with nonlocal goods in fairly similar proportions across age categories. When all nonperishable goods are considered, regardless of whether they are nonlocal or local in origin, the proportion of men buried with goods increases with age. Rather than suggesting that men gained status as they aged I believe that during the Late Woodland period their status shifted with age based on the types of grave goods interred with men upon burial. Young male graves contained mostly marine shell and stone tools, whereas older males were interred with marine shell, stone tools, smoking pipes, copper ornaments, viperidae fangs, carnivore tooth pendants, and tools manufactured from carnivore bones. One older male burial at the Crab Orchard site also contained a bone mask made from the maxilla bone (snout) of a wolf (see MacCord and Buchanan 1980:Figure 12). Many of the goods interred with older men appear to be more ritual in nature; perhaps representative of life statuses that were not available to younger men. The smoking of pipes, for example, was associated primarily with ritual, not pleasure, during this period in time (Nassaney 2000:423–424). Venomous snakes were used in healing rituals (Lefler 1967:134–135, 228) and snake fangs were used in ritual and medicinal scarification (Lefler 1967:232; Swanton 1946:784). Carnivorous animals, such as bear, mountain lion, and wolf, played important roles in ceremony, myth, and clan identify (Hudson 1976:139, 142–144, 196, 322).

During the Protohistoric period, the pattern for men changes dramatically. The mortuary goods interred with young men shifts from primarily marine shell at the Late Woodland Crab Orchard site to a whole array of items at the Protohistoric Trigg site, including marine shell, copper, toolkits, carnivore teeth and claw pendants, smoking pipes, ceramic vessels, carnivore bone tools, and toolkits. This lengthy list appears most similar in content to the goods interred with older men at the Crab Orchard site. Several of the young male burials also take on the appearance of the most well-provisioned older male burials of the Late Woodland period. I have suggested that many of the goods interred with older men during the Late Woodland period held ritual significance and represented connections to the spiritual world. Considering that young men at the Trigg site were being buried with many of the same types of goods as older men at the Crab Orchard site, had young men gained access to life statuses that once could only be obtained by older men?

One of the most striking changes in the Protohistoric period is the significantly greater proportion of young men buried with local and nonlocal goods, particularly marine shell. These data suggest to me that it was the younger men in the Trigg village who were the entrepreneurs in the deerskin trade, and that they were the ones who more actively pursued this new trade in processed hides as a way to gain access to nonlocal, status-marking goods. The acquisition and redistribution, or gifting, of nonlocal materials would have conveyed individual and household wealth and prestige to others within the village and local community. If young men brought the majority of the nonlocal goods into the Trigg community, it is likely that young men made some of the decisions about how to use these goods. It is just as likely that kinship relations dictated some decisions about how to use these materials (cf., Sahlins 1972:185–276). For example, the distribution of nonlocal goods in mortuary contexts is evidence that many of these items were given to children or perhaps to female kin who then gave these objects to children. Some nonlocal goods may have also been given directly to older male relatives to whom the young men had kin obligations.

Generosity played an important role in the social politics of many Native American societies (Collier 1988:74; Sahlins 1972:207; Trigger 1990:136–137). The young men at the Trigg site who gave gifts of marine shell, copper, and glass can be viewed as working within traditional systems that bound together generosity, respect, authority, and social obligations (cf., Mauss 1925). Not all nonlocal goods were given away, however. One young man retained a large copper gorget upon burial, perhaps the most impressive copper object recovered from the site, although the decision to bury this item with the young man ultimately fell upon another individual. By being generous, young men gained greater status than they would have had they hoarded these goods. Moreover, their actions did not outright defy traditional paths to prestige or existing political systems. By keeping some, but not all, of the nonlocal goods they obtained through interregional trade, young men may have sought to strike a balance in their behavior that did not blatantly challenge existing systems of authority but that still allowed them to gain greater social standing, and even power, within their communities.

6 Understanding Cultural Change in the Protohistoric Southern Appalachian Highlands

Changes in economic organization and mortuary practices in the Appalachian Highlands of southwestern Virginia during the Protohistoric period provide new insights into how participation in the seventeenth century deerskin trade initially altered Native American social relations and political systems. Understanding what motivated hide production for trade and how the nonlocal goods acquired in exchange for deerskins were used is central to understanding Native American cultural change in the historic era. Based on the patterns observed in the faunal remains, artifact assemblages, and mortuary materials, I have argued that several specific changes occurred within some Protohistoric Native American communities in southwestern Virginia. Deer exploitation and venison consumption increased. Hunting strategies became more selective toward deer whose hides would bring the most competitive exchange rates on the commercial market. Deer carcass skinning techniques reflected an attention to detail that at times was geared toward preserving maximum hide size. The manufacture and use of hide-working tools increased. And, nonlocal materials (i.e., marine shell, copper, and glass beads) show a marked increase in the quantities obtained. These data provide multiple lines of evidence that economic activities were intensified in order to produce surplus deerskins, which in turn were converted to nonlocal, socially valued goods through interregional trade and gift exchanges.

Deerskin Production for Trade

The question of who produced hides for trade is difficult to answer using the current data. Was deerskin processing a task performed primarily by women, largely by men, or by both sexes? Ethnohistoric literature specific to the Appalachian Highlands of southwestern Virginia provides no concrete evidence as to who within households produced deerskins, and a survey of ethnohistoric accounts from the greater study region only lengthens the list of possible scenarios. Hide production in Creek society, for example, rested exclusively on women (Braund 1993:68; Perdue 1998:71). Algonquian women also tanned deerskins, but during the summer months men might have participated in hide dressing as well (Rountree 1989:44, 1998:16). Among the Cherokee, the task of deerskin processing, like deer hunting, was the responsibility of the men in the village (Perdue 1998:71). Both men and women dressed hides prior to European contact in other southeastern Native American societies, but during historic times deerskin production shifted to women (Swanton 1946:445). Additionally, some native groups in North Carolina employed the labor of their "slaves and sorry Hunters" to dress hides for trade (Lefler 1967:217).

The archaeological data collected in this study on hide processing similarly contributes no definitive answer to this specific question; however, a hide-working tool found in a mortuary context adds a small piece to the larger puzzle. Out of more than 500 burials from the three archaeological sites (Crab Orchard, Hoge, and Trigg) only one grave yielded a bone hide-working tool. A beamer, contained within a toolkit, was buried with a young man 20–25 years old at the Protohistoric Trigg site. Considering that gender-specific grave goods representative of male and female activities have been identified in mortuary assemblages elsewhere in the southern Middle Atlantic and Southeast (Eastman 2001; Rodning 2001), it is quite possible that the inclusion of a hide-working tool reflects a task once preformed by the deceased individual. These data are intriguing, at the very least, if not suggestive that some men (especially young men) processed deerskins, although the find does not provide evidence that only men dressed deerskins nor does it refute the very likely possibility that women also processed hides.

Hide processing likely took place within the basic domestic unit, the household, during both the Late Woodland and Protohistoric periods because the task was necessary to fulfill basic needs for clothing and shelter. This factor makes it even more difficult to pinpoint which households intensified hide production for trade since, theoretically, most households processed hides for personal use. The spatial distribution of processing-related activities indicates, as expected, that hide processing took place within most, and likely all, households at the Protohistoric Trigg site. It also appears that hide production intensified village-wide, although this observation is based on negative evidence since no specialized activity areas associated with intensive processing could be detected within the village. This might well have been the case, however, considering the distribution of nonlocal grave goods. If only a few households intensified processing activities to produce surplus hides for trade, I would expect nonlocal materials to show a fairly restricted distribution in burials. Instead, nonlocal goods show a broad distribution among the Protohistoric burial population. More people used nonlocal goods during the seventeenth century, suggesting that the proportion of the population exchanging and gifting these items had increased as well.

Participation in this interregional trade in hides, furs, and nonlocal goods would have afforded certain persons or social groups a new opportunity to heighten their own social standing within the community. Although asymmetrical social relations existed within some Late Woodland Native American societies, European colonization acted as a catalyst in the historic development, negotiation, and expression of these social, political, and economic processes. I contend that the ability to acquire nonlocal goods through the surplus production and exchange of deerskins provided seventeenth-century entrepreneurs, such as the young men of the Trigg village, with a new and effective way to enhance their prestige, increase their authority, and cultivate local and regional alliances through the public display, reciprocal giving, and exchange of socially valued objects. Trading deerskins provided, in effect, a new route of social mobility, although as I argued in the previous chapter, the actions of the young men seem to have been balanced between working within and challenging traditional sociopolitical systems.

Continuing with this scenario, it is quite possible that the social and political agendas of these young entrepreneurs stimulated economic activities toward productive intensification. Intensified production can be accomplished by increasing the labor output of existing workers or by enlarging the number of workers who contribute their labor to a household. Polygyny, adoption, caring for widows, and taking in orphans allow the domestic labor force to be expanded (Collier 1988:74). Among the Blackfoot of the northern Plains, polygyny became a more common practice in the eighteenth and nineteenth centuries as the fur trade placed greater demands on women's labor (Lewis 1942). In his defense of polygyny to Catholic missionaries who opposed the practice, one Blackfoot chief remarked that his eight wives could dress 150 buffalo hides in a year whereas one wife could produce ten at best (Lewis 1942:39). The chief's statement regarding the production potential of his wives emphasizes that cooperation among several workers produces more surplus than a single laborer working alone.

Expanding the household unit, regardless of how it might be accomplished (i.e., polygyny, adoption, and such), would take time to implement and the benefit of additional workers would not be realized immediately. The quickest way to create surplus would be to increase the amount of labor that existing workers contributed to production. It is conceivable, although purely speculative, that young men in collaboration with other family members and kin gave a greater portion of their labor hours to deerskin production activities during the Protohistoric period than they had in the past. This hypothesis provides one explanation for why production activities appear to have intensified village-wide at the Trigg site. Young men, whether single or married, would have been present in households throughout the village, which would result in intensive production appearing to be broadly distributed archaeologically. If productive intensification occurred within a few select households, perhaps those of leaders or persons aspiring to the status, then I would expect processing activities to have shown a more restricted distribution or for locales of intensive production to have been more clearly discernable in the archaeological record.

Social Status and Gender Relations

In the concluding section of the previous chapter, I focused my discussion on the patterns apparent in the distribution of nonlocal grave goods among the two adult male burial populations and my interpretations of these data. I did this not to obscure or omit the contributions of Native American women (cf., Klein and Ackerman 1995), but to emphasize my belief that it was the young men of the Protohistoric Trigg village who were the entrepreneurs in the deerskin trade. There is much more to be said about the mortuary data, however. Two patterns that need to be elaborated upon are the increase in subadults buried with nonlocal goods and the decrease in adult females buried with these materials during the Protohistoric period.

When I began my research I did not intend to embark upon a discussion of changing gender relations, yet in the end this is a topic I find most intriguing. Participation in the deerskin and fur trades initially influenced and eventually restructured the gendered division of labor and production within Native American households (Devens 1992; Kidwell 1995; Leacock 1978; Perdue 1998; Perry 1979; Sleeper-Smith 2000; Van Kirk 1983; White 1999), yet the cultural specifics were neither unilateral nor unidirectional. In the southern Appalachian Highlands, the fewer women buried with nonlocal goods during the Protohistoric period stands in marked contrast to the increase in these materials buried with everyone else in the community (i.e., infants, children, adolescents, and men). Do these changes reflect changing attitudes among women or toward women? Are they representative of a lowering in status or a shift in status? Before the meaning of these patterns can be speculated upon, it is first necessary to diverge briefly into what is historically known about the inception and initial development of the deerskin trade in Virginia. This will lay the foundation needed to better interpret the archaeological evidence.

European colonists frequently noted the value and abundance of animal hides and furs offered in exchange for foreign goods by the native North Americans they encountered on their initial travels of the country (Quinn and Quinn 1973:53; Tyler 1907:108). Although the extent and frequency of these early, informal exchanges in deerskins and other furs is not clear from the historic documents, the acquisition and export of pelts likely remained of little concern to more than a few Virginia colonists during the first quarter of the seventeenth century. Colonists at Jamestown, the first permanent English settlement in North America established in 1607 near present-day Williamsburg, struggled to overcome famine and disease during this early period. When intercultural relations were amicable, trade with Native Americans focused primarily on acquiring corn and other foodstuffs for survival, not commodities for export (Kelso 1995; Robinson 1979:25–26).

During the sixteen-teens, following several years of mutual hostilities, English relations with local Algonquian groups were generally peaceful (Fausz 1985:241–244). This period of peace ended abruptly in 1622 when the Powhatans and allied neighboring Algonquian groups launched a strategic attack on English settlements to revenge the murder of their religious leader who had been killed by a colonist several weeks earlier and to thwart further colonial encroachment upon Algonquian lands (Fausz 1985:244–245). The assault, which targeted plantations and farmsteads along a 100-mile stretch of the James River, killed about 350 persons, more than one-quarter of the colony's population at that time. English retaliation for the strike was immediate and long lasting, leaving the next decade characterized largely by intercultural violence.

During this period, the Virginia colony restricted trade to those who held a government-issued license. In 1627, William Clairborne was given permission to "truck with the Indians for furs, skins, and other commodities" (Phillips 1961:163). Clairborne established his first trading post in 1631 at Kent Island in the northern Chesapeake Bay, followed soon after by a second fort on Palmer's Island located north of Kent Island at the mouth of the Susquehannock River (Fausz 1983:18–19). An alliance carefully cultivated with the Susquehannocks, native peoples who inhabited the lower Susquehanna Valley in south-central Pennsylvania, brought profitable pelts to Clairborne and his enterprise prospered (Fausz 1983:20). Deerskins undoubtedly entered into exchanges between Clairborne and his Native American trading partners, but at this northern latitude beaver and other small fur-bearing animals grew the thick coats valued as luxury items in Great Britain and thus these species dominated the trade.

By the early 1630s trade in deerskins had become prevalent enough to warrant recognition from government officials in Virginia. In that year the governor prohibited the export of deerskins in an attempt to build and promote a leather industry within the colony itself (Phillips 1961:164). During the next three decades, disgruntled deerskin traders and local leather manufacturers battled in colonial courts, each group fighting to sway the law toward a statute that would improve their own financial gain. Traders relied on the exportation of hides and furs for their livelihood, while colony tanners benefited from pelts remaining in the Americas. These legal contestations resulted in laws being repealed and reinstated numerous times (Henning 1823a:174, 199, 307, 314, 488, 497). Legislative conflicts did not deter all hide exportation, however. Some merchants attempted to continue with their export endeavors by seeking ways around the direct violation of pertinent laws (Phillips 1961:164). Finally, in 1659, the government ruled that exporting hides would prove more profitable than supporting the colonial leather industry and removed the prohibition on hide exportation, opening the market for free trade (Henning 1823a:525).

Prior to the mid-seventeenth century few Euro-Americans ventured beyond the haven of colonial settlements clustered along the southern Chesapeake Bay and its tributaries. The relative immobility of colonial merchants meant that Native Americans had to bring their deerskins to colonial towns or trade their hides with native groups that lived within the vicinity of these settlements (Robinson 1979:55). Whether or not trading took place, and the frequency with which these activities occurred, involved a number of factors, including the ever-changing state of intercultural relations. In the 1640s, the Virginia government began to encourage westward explorations. Their support waned in 1644 following another collective attack by Algonquians on outlying colonial settlements south of the James River (Phillips 1961:167; Robinson 1979:55). The attack killed about 400 colonists from a population that now exceeded 10,000 persons (Gleach 1997:175).

Trading operations in Virginia saw a key development in 1645 when the colonial government established forts along the four main southern rivers (Phillips 1961:167). The strategic placement of these forts at the fall line, an area of rough waters that separates the Coastal Plain and Piedmont, was intended to strengthen military operations within the colony following the 1644 Algonquian attack. However, a peace treaty, signed in 1646, made the forts obsolete in terms of providing protection for colonists and thus too great an expenditure of public monies for the government to continue to subsidize (Briceland 1987:8). The government transferred the forts and the responsibility of their upkeep to private entrepreneurs, who quickly realized they were in an ideal position to support westward explorations and expand trade

(Briceland 1987:8). The new proprietors were able to focus their interests on commercial opportunities other than farming, from which "the profitable business of the southern 'deerskin' trade was born" (Binford 1991:155). Embarking from these forts, colonial traders began to make annual excursions into western Virginia to bargain their wares for hides and furs at native villages. By the mid- to late seventeenth century, the deerskin trade was well established in the Middle Atlantic and Southeast (Crane 1928; Martin 1994; Parrish 1972; Stine 1990; Stubbs 1960), with Carolina merchants entering into the commerce in the 1670s following the establishment of Charlestown (Robinson 1979:86; see also Gallay 2002).

Native Americans residing in the southern Appalachian Highlands during the early to mid-seventeenth century, at the time the Protohistoric Trigg site was occupied, would have been insulated from both regular and direct contact with the English. Colonial traders were certainly not traveling to native settlements located in southwestern Virginia, more than 200 miles from the safety of their towns and farmsteads. If face-to-face interactions ever occurred, it would have been a rare event and the meeting would have taken place at a more easterly location. Based on the history of colonial explorations in Virginia, it is reasonable to assume that the Trigg site residents acquired most, if not all, nonlocal materials through exchanges with other native groups who had closer or direct contact with Euro-American traders. John Lawson observed such native middlemen during the early eighteenth century. He recalled that the native peoples he visited in eastern North Carolina manufactured goods such as baskets and pipes for trade with which they were able to acquire "raw Skins with the Hair on, which our neighboring *Indians* bring to their towns" (Lefler 1967:217). It was at these easterly towns that "slaves and sorry Hunters" were made to dress hides, completing their preparation for trade to colonial merchants.

It has been suggested that the status of women in the context of the deerskin and fur trades depended, to some extent, upon the structure of their contributions and the nature of participation (Leacock 1978; Perry 1979). Based on information gleaned from historic documents in conjunction with archaeological evidence, it is possible to characterize the deerskin trade in the southern Appalachian Highlands during the early to mid-seventeenth century as likely involving small-scale intensive production, possibly resulting from additional labor hours devoted to processing activities. In exchange for surplus hides, European-manufactured and nonlocal native-made goods were obtained through interregional trade and gift-exchanges. At this early period in time, Native Americans in southwestern Virginia likely traded their hides to other native groups rather than directly to colonial merchants. I have argued that the sociopolitical aspirations of young men were a motivating factor in the surplus production of hides and that they actively cultivated the interregional trade of deerskins. This does not exclude the possibility, however, that women also influenced or participated in trading activities.

Returning to the question posed earlier, why are fewer women buried with valued, nonlocal goods during the Protohistoric period while the proportion of infants, children, adolescents, and men buried with these materials increases? According to Eleanor Leacock (1978), a decline in the status of women can be seen when women begin to lose control of the goods they produce, which often occurs in association with the transition from production for use to production for trade. Among the Ojibwa, for example, increased involvement in the fur trade altered many of the production activities of women, which diminished their direct contribution to the community (Devens 1992). A growing demand for trade furs combined with an increased reliance on European goods, including cloth and ready-made garments, lessened the need for women to produce hides and furs for clothing. Because trade now supplied basic necessities women reoriented their labor toward the processing of furs for the Euro-American market. Women no longer produced usable goods outright; instead, dependent upon their husbands and male kin for European manufactures, they processed furs that the men then controlled through trade (Devens 1992:16–17).

This perspective has been recently challenged by Bruce White (1999) and others. White contends that the fur trade provided Ojibwa women and men with diverse opportunities to participate in trade, giving each different but equally influential roles. In the northern fur trade that operated in the Great Lakes region women regularly bartered foodstuffs, and sometimes furs, for Euro-American goods and took an active role in the selection of goods acquired through trade by their husbands (B. White 1999:123). Native women often married fur traders, in which capacity they acted as liaisons, or cultural mediators, between their kin and the trader's world. These women also made important contributions to the trade as bilingual interpreters, backcountry navigators, and food producers (Brown 1980; Van Kirk 1983). In addition, some women became independent traders whose strategic kinship alliances, both familial and fictive, gave them substantial power within the greater fur trade community (Sleeper-Smith 2000).

In the southern Appalachian Highlands, the surplus production and trade of deerskins was just beginning in the early to mid-seventeenth century when native peoples inhabited the Protohistoric Trigg site. Native Americans in this region remained distanced, geographically and economically, from extensive involvement with Euro-Americans at that time and for several decades there-

after. It is unlikely that women would have given up power over their labor
or the partial products of their labor without some larger force, such as im-
mersion in a mercantile economy, prompting this change. Rather than viewing the decline in women buried with prestige goods as a lowering in status,
I believe that the status of women shifted during the Protohistoric period.
But, shifted how?

In the context of European contact, Native American women have sometimes been described as the "guardians of tradition" (Braund 1990; Devens
1992; Kidwell 1995). Native women associated themselves with cultural traditions as a way to defend their own status and interests during times when
social solidarity and political orders were being threatened by the broad-
reaching effects of European colonization. Within many precontact Native
North American societies women and men held complementary roles that
had equally important responsibilities attached to each. Interactions with
male-dominated European societies skewed this balance, resulting in women's
positions being devalued in native society. It is possible that some women in
the southern Appalachian Highlands disapproved of the changes they observed taking place within their communities and made a conscious decision
to disassociate themselves from objects obtained through trading activities.

Differences in the distribution of grave goods among women in the Late
Woodland and Protohistoric periods suggests a certain amount of conserva-
tiveness associated with adult female burials during the latter period. The proportion of women buried with locally available goods, for example, doubles
from 8 percent in the Late Woodland period to 16 percent in the Protohistoric
period, while at the same time the frequency of women buried with nonlocal
materials decreases by about one-third. Furthermore, when nonlocal goods
do occur in Protohistoric female burials, the material type leans toward the
conservative end of the continuum of nonlocal goods. Marine shell, on the
one hand, could be obtained in fairly large quantities throughout the late
Late Woodland and Protohistoric periods. It can be viewed as a more conservative good because it was available through long-distance exchange both
before and after European contact. Glass beads, on the other hand, were
brought to the Americas by Europeans. It was the one new material type to
enter funerary assemblages in the southern Appalachian Highlands during
the period studied. Because of its newness, glass beads can be viewed as a
less conservative material within the spectrum of nonlocal goods available
to native peoples in southwestern Virginia. Copper resides in the middle of
this continuum, between marine shell and glass beads, in that it was available in its purest form in very limited amounts to elite individuals during
the Late Woodland period, but became more readily available with the influx
of European copper-alloys during the historic era. At the Protohistoric Trigg

site, marine shell was the most common nonlocal good to be interred with women. Only one woman was buried with a nonlocal material other than shell, and this individual received copper beads upon burial. Not a single woman was buried with glass beads, although these items were present in four adult male burials.

Another possible explanation for why fewer women received nonlocal goods upon burial during the Protohistoric period considers the context of these materials in mortuary rituals. Culturally prescribed behavior dictates proper treatment of the dead, including how to inter the deceased, perform funerary rites, and express grief and other emotions (Metcalf and Huntington 1991). According to Aubrey Cannon, situations of social change often "required increased efforts to establish, maintain, and enhance status through material display" (1989:443). Mortuary rituals thus become social investments that represent competitive expressions of status consciously manipulated by living social groups (Cannon 1989; Parker Pearson 1984). The decisions to bury certain goods with specific people were made by living persons whose actions conveyed as much information about their own interests and aspirations as they did about the qualities of the deceased (Brown 1995; Hutchinson and Aragon 2002; O'Shea 1996).

While a woman would have had limited influence over her own funeral, her female kin (e.g., mothers, sisters, daughters) would have been intimately involved in the process and, as such, would have provided a women's perspective on the matter. This is not to suggest that all women, regardless of age or life position, think the same; rather, I am proposing that if something was culturally important to a woman, as an individual, or to women, as a collective, there would have been other female kin who knew this and could ensure that the appropriate steps were taken to meet the expectations of, or requests made by, the deceased in life. Women surely made and influenced funerary-related decisions associated with the burial of their children, husbands, brothers, sons, and fathers. At the Protohistoric Trigg site, the distribution of nonlocal goods in burial contexts indicates that during the Protohistoric period subadults were twice as likely, and adult males a third more likely, to be buried with nonlocal goods than adult females. Women may have been buried with nonlocal goods less often than their children and male kin, but since the decisions behind such actions involved women perhaps a more fruitful approach to explain the meaning behind these patterns lies again in reframing the focus of inquiry to who was, rather than who was not, being buried with nonlocal goods.

The reason why more men, especially *young* men, received nonlocal goods upon burial is clearly linked to their ability to obtain these items through interregional trade and gift exchanges. It is interesting to note that at the

Protohistoric Trigg site *young women* were twice as likely to be buried with
nonlocal goods compared with mature and older women. This trend might
be associated with the life status and age-related reproductive powers of
young women since young women were in their prime childbearing years
and, as such, contributed to society through both production and reproduc-
tion, the latter of which becomes more biologically challenging for women as
they get older. The Late Woodland burial data support this hypothesis in that
young women at the Crab Orchard site were also interred with nonlocal
goods much more frequently than mature and older women. Another possible, and at the same time complementary, explanation for why more young
women received nonlocal goods upon burial compared to mature and older
women during the Protohistoric period considers the marital and familiar
associations of young women (as wives and sisters) with young men and,
by extension, the potential of their collaborative efforts in surplus hide production.

Besides young men, subadults are the second most likely age group to be
buried with nonlocal goods during the Protohistoric period. Subadults obvi-
ously did not acquire nonlocal goods themselves, but rather they would have
received these items in life or upon burial as gifts from older male and female
kin. This new emphasis on burying more subadults with greater amounts of
material wealth suggests that changes were occurring in the way society
viewed infants, children, and adolescents. At the Protohistoric Trigg site,
subadults comprise more than half (56 percent) of the burial population; an
increase of more than 20 percent from the Late Woodland period. If mortuary rituals are viewed as competitive expressions of status and status aspirations, then it is possible that family status came to be represented more often
in subadult graves because their deaths had become more frequent. Since
subadults died more often during the Protohistoric period, increased social
investment in their burial would have provided more frequent opportunities
to display family wealth through mortuary ritual.

It is also possible that family (both immediate and extended), rather than
a larger social group such as clan, became a more important social and economic category following the inception of the historic deerskin trade. Because children represent a continuation of the family (i.e., the next genera-
tion) they may have been associated more closely with family status. Among
the Huron of the Georgian Bay area in southern Ontario, certain families
within a community held exclusive rights to specific trade routes. Whoever
had discovered the route claimed these rights, and trading for furs along a
route without permission of the proprietary family violated Huron custom
(Trigger 1976:65). Whether or not such trading rules existed prior to the
French fur trade is unknown; regardless, this example demonstrates that the

family group was a socially important and economically viable entity during the early historic period. In the Appalachian Highlands of southwestern Virginia, trade in deerskins may have stimulated competition among different families within the Protohistoric Trigg community. As a result, the distinction of one's family status may have been more important than clan or village associations. Rather than viewing the increase in subadults buried with non-local goods as an elevation in the status of children, it seems more likely that greater elaboration in funerary rituals for children, who in essence embodied the family, can be better explained as displaying the status ambitions of bereaving family members.

Conclusions

For those involved in the deerskin trade, Native American and Euro-American alike, the importance of incorporating native peoples from the southern Appalachian Highlands into this transatlantic commerce became a critical and unavoidable step to ensure the commercial vitality of the trade into the eighteenth century. The continued depopulation of white-tailed deer in eastern regions, along with increased competition for good hunting grounds, forced Euro-American merchants to rely more heavily on deerskins procured by native hunters from western settlements to meet the growing demands of the overseas leather industry. William Byrd I a prominent Virginia trader in the late seventeenth century, understood the importance of supplying goods that complied with the demands of his Native American trading partners, many of whom occupied these western regions (Tinling 1977). Whether or not an item met their standards figured prominently in the acceptance or rejection of his trade goods. Requests for specific sizes, colors, and types of merchandise were recurrent themes in the letters Byrd wrote to his London suppliers. He observed that the Native Americans he traded with wanted small not large white beads (Tinling 1977:63, 66), preferred dark not light blue cloth (Tinling 1977:30, 31, 41), and refused to purchase small hoes (Tinling 1977:57). This new native economy, one that emphasized hunting for commercial hide production along with increased competition for European commodities and the broader impacts of European colonization led to some substantial changes in Native American societies by the late seventeenth and eighteenth centuries. These changes redirected trade networks (Usner 1992), altered political alliances and gave rise to the development of political factions and middlemen (Martin 1994; Ward and Davis 1993; Waselkov 1993), and reshaped gender relations (Perdue 1998) and cultural belief systems (Martin 1978, for an alternative perspective see Hudson 1981).

It is not the demise of one thing and the rise of another that I have sought to understand in this study; but, rather the balancing of the familiar with the recently discovered—the "something new" that can emerge from intercultural contacts. My research into the use of deer, deerskins, and nonlocal goods in the Appalachian Highlands of southwestern Virginia provides a glimpse into the very beginnings of historic era cultural changes within Native American societies. During the Protohistoric period, surplus deerskins provided the material means to obtain valued, nonlocal goods that conveyed individual and family wealth and prestige to others within the community. Those who traded in deerskins expanded their access to wealth by exploiting this new opportunity to participate in a growing trade in hides, furs, and nonlocal goods. The results of this study suggest that deerskin production for trade initially involved small-scale intensive production, possibly resulting from additional labor hours devoted to processing activities. I have argued that the sociopolitical aspirations of young men were a motivating factor in the surplus production and trade of hides, although this does not exclude the likelihood that women also influenced and participated in these activities. Social differences also received greater material expression during the Protohistoric period, and I have presented several possible hypotheses to explain the uneven distribution of nonlocal status-marking goods in mortuary contexts.

For me this study has raised as many questions as it has attempted to answer. How did, for example, the declining consumption of bear affect historic Native American medicinal practices, ritual, and religion? Did young men gain access during the Protohistoric period to life statuses that once could only be obtained by older men as hinted at in the mortuary data? Is there other archaeological evidence that suggests the family unit became a more important social and economic category as lifeways became more enmeshed in the deerskin trade? And, what effects might this have had on community sociopolitical organization? One avenue for future research is to examine the current data more closely at the household level rather than considering the village as a whole. Elucidating relationships within and between household units may help to clarify, or refute, some of the interpretations presented in the current research. Answering these questions and others will also require information from new contexts dated contemporaneous with, earlier, and later than the current study sites. I am not suggesting that archaeologists must excavate more sites to achieve this goal; instead, the reexamination of existing archaeological collections is an excellent way to obtain these data, and one that has proven to be extremely productive in the current study.

References Cited

Ambrose, Stanley H., and Lynette Norr

1993 Experimental Evidence for the Relationship of the Carbon Isotope Ratios of Whole Diet and Dietary Protein to Those of Bone Collagen and Carbonate. In *Prehistoric Human Bone: Archaeology at the Molecular Level,* edited by Joseph B. Lambert and Gisela Grupe, pp. 1–37. Springer-Verlag, Berlin.

American Ornithologists' Union

1998 *Check-List of North American Birds: The Species of Birds of North America from the Arctic through Panama, Including the West Indies and Hawaiian Islands.* 7th ed. Committee on Classification and Nomenclature, American Ornithologists' Union, Washington, D.C.

Arnold, Jeanne E.

1991 Transformation of a Regional Economy: Sociopolitical Evolution in the Production of Valuables in Southern California. *Antiquity* 65:953–962.

1996 Organizational Transformation: Power and Labor among Complex Hunter-Gatherers and Other Intermediate Societies. In *Emergent Complexity: The Evolution of Intermediate Societies,* edited by Jeanne E. Arnold, pp. 59–73. Archaeological Series No. 9. International Monographs in Prehistory, Ann Arbor.

Baker, Rollin H.

1984 Origin, Classification and Distribution. In *White-Tailed Deer: Ecology and Management,* edited by Lowell K. Halls, pp. 1–18. Stackpole Books, Harrisburg, Pennsylvania.

Barber, Michael B.

n.d. Late Woodland Vertebrate Faunal Utilization Patterns in the South Ridge and Valley of Virginia: Changes through Time. Preservation Technologies, Inc., Salem, Virginia.

1989a Human Prehistory beyond the Blue Ridge: A Brief Introduction. Revised version of a paper presented at The Blue Ridge Symposium, Roanoke College, Virginia, February 29, 1980.

1989b Preliminary Vertebrate Faunal Analysis: The Hall Site, Montgomery County, Virginia. Report on file with the Virginia Department of Historic Resources, Richmond.

1999 Faunal Analysis: 44RN2. Report on file with the Virginia Department of Historic Resources, Richmond.

2003   *The Late Woodland Dan River People: A Social Reconstruction Based on the Study of Bone Tools at a Regional Scale.* Ph.D. dissertation. University Microfilms International, Ann Arbor.

Barber, Michael B., Michael F. Barber, and Eugene B. Barfield

1997   The Hurt Power Plant Site (44py144), Pittsylvania County, Virginia: A Regional Perspective on the Early Contact Period Based on Bone Tool Analysis. Paper presented at the annual meeting of the Middle Atlantic Archaeological Conference, Ocean City, Maryland.

Barber, Michael B., Michael F. Barber, and Christopher Bowen

1996   Phase III Excavations at the Hurt Power Plant Site, Pittsylvania County, Virginia: A Protohistoric Village on the Middle Roanoke (Staunton) River. Preservation Technologies Inc., Salem, Virginia. Report on file with the Virginia Department of Historic Resources, Richmond.

Barber, Michael B., and Eugene B. Barfield

2000   The Late Woodland in the Environs of Saltville: A Case for Petty Chiefdom Development. *Journal of Middle Atlantic Archaeology* 16:117–132.

Barber, Michael B., and John Baroody

1977   Analysis of the Vertebrate Faunal Remains from the Shannon Site, Montgomery County, Virginia. *Archeological Society of Virginia Quarterly Bulletin* 31(3):101–113.

Barber, Michael B., and Celia Reed

1994   Analysis of the Vertebrate Fauna [from the Legget Site]. *Archeological Society of Virginia Quarterly Bulletin* 49(3):89–120.

Barber, Michael B., Todd N. Solberg, and Eugene B. Barfield

1996   The Composition of Copper Recovered from Contact Native American Sites in the Lower Piedmont and Southern Ridge and Valley, Virginia. *Virginia Journal of Science* 47(1):9–18.

Barfield, Eugene B., and Michael B. Barber

1992   Archaeological and Ethnographic Evidence of Subsistence in Virginia during the Late Woodland Period. In *Middle and Late Woodland Research in Virginia: A Synthesis,* edited by Theodore R. Reinhart and Mary Ellen N. Hodges, pp. 225–248. Special Publication 29. Archeological Society of Virginia, Richmond.

Bassett, John Spencer (editor)

1901   *The Writings of "Colonial William Byrd of Westover in Virginia ESQ^R."* Doubleday, Page, and Company, New York.

Behrensmeyer, Anna K.

1978   Taphonomic and Ecologic Information from Bone Weathering. *Paleobiology* 4(2):150–162.

1991   Terrestrial Vertebrate Accumulations. In *Taphonomy: Releasing the Data Locked in the Fossil Record,* edited by Peter A. Allison and Derek E. G. Briggs, pp. 291–335. Plenum Press, New York.

Bender, Barbara
   1978   Gatherer-Hunter to Farmer: A Social Perspective. *World Archaeology* 10(2):204–222.

Benthall, Joseph L.
   1969   *Archeological Investigation of the Shannon Site, Montgomery County, Virginia.* Virginia State Library, Richmond.

Binford, Lewis R.
   1967   Smudge Pits and Hide Smoking: The Use of Analogy in Archaeological Reasoning. *American Antiquity* 32(1):1–12.
   1978   *Nunamiut Ethnoarchaeology.* Academic Press, New York.
   1981   *Bones: Ancient Men and Modern Myths.* Academic Press, New York.
   1991   *Cultural Diversity among Aboriginal Cultures of Coastal Virginia and North Carolina.* Garland, New York.

Bishop, J. Leander
   1864   *A History of American Manufactures, 1608–1860.* 3rd ed. E. Young and Company, Philadelphia.

Blanton, Richard, and Gary Feinman
   1984   The Mesoamerican World System. *American Anthropologist* 86:673–682.

Bowen, Joanne
   1996   Foodways in the 18th-Century Chesapeake. In *The Archaeology of 18th-Century Virginia,* edited by Theodore R. Reinhart, pp. 87–130. Special Publication No. 35, Archeological Society of Virginia, Richmond.

Boyd, C. Clifford
   1993   The Trigg site (44MY3) and Other Late Woodland/Contact Period Sites along the New River Valley in Southwest Virginia. Paper presented at the Southeastern Archaeological Conference, Raleigh, North Carolina.

Boyd, C. Clifford, Jr., Donna C. Boyd, Michael B. Barber, and David A. Hubbard, Jr.
   2001   Southwest Virginia's Burial Caves: Skeletal Biology, Mortuary Behavior, and Legal Issues. *Midcontinental Journal of Archaeology* 26(2):219-231.

Boyd, Donna C., and C. Clifford Boyd
   1992   Late Woodland Mortuary Variability in Virginia. In *Middle and Late Woodland Research in Virginia: A Synthesis,* edited by Theodore R. Reinhart and Mary Ellen N. Hodges, pp. 249–275. Special Publication No. 29. Archeological Society of Virginia, Richmond.
   2001   Human Skeletal Remains. In *Contributions to the Archaeology of Southwestern Virginia: A Volume Honoring the Author Emory Eugene Jones, Jr., of Bluefield, West Virginia,* pp. 183–191. Special Publication No. 40. Archeological Society of Virginia, Richmond.

Bradley, James W.
   1977   The Pompey Center Site: The Impact of European Trade Goods, 1600–

1620. *Archaeological Society of New York, William M. Beauchamp Chapter Bulletin* 2(1):1–19.

Brain, Jeffrey P.
1979   *Tunica Treasure.* Peabody Museum of Archaeology and Ethnology, Harvard University, Cambridge, Massachusetts; The Peabody Museum of Salem, Salem, Massachusetts.

Braun, E. Lucy
1964   *Deciduous Forests of Eastern North America.* Hafner Publishing, New York.

Braund, Kathryn E. Holland
1990   Guardians of Tradition and Handmaidens to Change: Women's Roles in Creek Economic and Social Life during the Eighteenth Century. *American Indian Quarterly* 14(3):239–258.
1993   *Deerskins and Duffels: The Creek Indian Trade with Anglo-America, 1685–1815.* University of Nebraska Press, Lincoln.

Briceland, Alan Vance
1987   *Westward from Virginia: The Exploration of the Virginia-Carolina Frontier, 1650–1710.* University of Virginia Press, Charlottesville.

Brown, James A.
1995   On Mortuary Analysis—With Special Reference to the Saxe-Binford Research Program. In *Regional Approaches to Mortuary Analysis,* edited by Lane Beck Anderson, pp. 3–26. Plenum Press, New York.

Brown, Jennifer S. H.
1980   *Strangers in Blood: Fur Trade Company Families in Indian Country.* University of Oklahoma Press, Norman.

Brumfiel, Elizabeth M.
1987   Elite and Utilitarian Crafts in the Aztec State. In *Specialization, Exchange, and Complex Societies,* edited by Elizabeth M. Brumfiel and Timothy K. Earle, pp. 102–118. Cambridge University Press, Cambridge.

Buchanan, William T.
1984   *The Trigg Site, City of Radford, Virginia.* Archeological Society of Virginia, Richmond.

Buikstra, Jane E.
1976   *Hopewell in the Lower Illinois Valley: A Regional Approach to the Study of Human Biological Variability and Prehistoric Behavior.* Scientific Papers No. 2. Northwestern University Archaeological Program, Evanston.
1981   Mortality Practices, Paleodemography and Paleopathology: A Case Study from the Koster Site (Illinois). In the *Archaeology of Death,* edited by Robert Chapman, Ian Kinnes, and Klavs Randsborg, pp. 123–132. Cambridge University Press, Cambridge.

Caldwell, Joseph R.
1951   Archaeological Investigations in Western Virginia. *Archeological Society of Virginia Quarterly Bulletin* 5(3).

Cannon, Aubrey
    1989   The Historical Dimension in Mortuary Expressions of Status and Sentiment. *Current Anthropology* 30(4):437–447.

Casteel, Richard W.
    1977   Characterization of Faunal Assemblages and the Minimum Number of Individuals Determined from Paired Elements: Continuing Problems in Archaeology. *Journal of Archaeological Science* 4:125–134.
    1978   Faunal Assemblages and the "Wiegemethose" or Weight Method. *Journal of Field Archaeology* 5:71–77.

Clarkson, L. A.
    1960   The Organization of the English Leather Industry in the Late Sixteenth and Seventeenth Centuries. *Economic History Review* 13(1):245–256.

Clayton, Lawrence A., Vernon James Knight, Jr., and Edward C. Moore (editors)
    1993   *The De Soto Chronicles: The Expedition of Hernando de Soto to North America, 1539–1543.* University of Alabama Press, Tuscaloosa.

Cleland, Charles E.
    1993   Economic and Adaptive Change among the Lake Superior Chippewa of the Nineteenth Century. In *Ethnohistory and Archaeology: Approaches to Postcontact Change in the Americas,* edited by J. Daniel Rogers and Samuel M. Wilson, pp. 111–122. Plenum Press, New York.

Coe, Joffre L.
    1995   *Town Creek Indian Mound.* University of North Carolina Press, Chapel Hill.

Collier, Jane Fishburne
    1988   *Marriage and Inequality in Classless Societies.* Stanford University Press, Stanford.

Collins, Joseph T., and Travis W. Taggart
    2002   *Standard Common and Current Scientific Names for North American Amphibians, Turtles, Reptiles and Crocodilians.* 5th ed. The Center for North American Herpetology, Lawrence, Kansas.

Crane, Verner W.
    1928   *The Southern Frontier, 1670–1732.* Duke University Press, Durham.

Cusick, James G. (editor)
    1998   *Studies in Culture Contact: Interaction, Culture Change, and Archaeology.* Occasional Paper No. 25. Center for Archaeological Investigations, Southern Illinois University, Carbondale.

Custer, Jay F.
    1986   Late Woodland Cultural Diversity in the Middle Atlantic: An Evolutionary Perspective. In *Late Woodland Cultures of the Middle Atlantic Region,* edited by Jay F. Custer, pp. 143–168. University of Delaware Press, Newark.

David, Bruno
    1990   How Was This Bone Burnt? In *Problem Solving in Taphonomy: Archaeo-*

logical and Palaeontological Studies from Europe, Africa, and Oceania, edited by I. Davidson and D. W. S. Solomon, pp. 65–79. Anthropology Museum Tempus, Vol. 2. University of Queensland, St. Lucia, Brisbane.

Davis, R. P. Stephen

1987   Pottery from the Fredericks, Wall, and Mitchum Sites. In *The Siouan Project: Seasons I and II,* edited by Roy S. Dickens, Jr., H. Trawick Ward, and R. P. Stephen Davis, Jr., pp. 185–215. Monograph Series No. 1. Research Laboratories of Anthropology, University of North Carolina, Chapel Hill.

Devens, Carol

1992   *Countering Colonialism: Native American Women and Great Lakes Missions, 1630–1900.* University of California Press, Berkeley.

Dickens, Roy S., Jr.

1985   The Form, Function, and Formation of Garbage-Filled Pits on Southeastern Aboriginal Sites: An Archaeobotanical Analysis. In *Structure and Process in Southeastern Archaeology,* edited by Roy S. Dickens, Jr., and H. Trawick Ward, pp. 34–59. University of Alabama Press, Tuscaloosa.

Dunham, Gary H.

1994   Common Ground, Contesting Visions: The Emergence of Burial Mound Ritual in Late Prehistoric Central Virginia. Ph.D. dissertation, Department of Anthropology, University of Virginia, Charlottesville.

Dunham, Gary H., Debra L. Gold, and Jeffrey L. Hantman

2003   Collective Burial in Late Prehistoric Virginia: Excavation and Analysis of the Rapidan Mound. *American Antiquity* 68(1):109–128.

Earle, Timothy K.

1987   Specialization and the Production of Wealth: Hawaiian Chiefdoms and the Inka Empire. In *Specialization, Exchange, and Complex Societies,* edited by Elizabeth M. Brumfiel and Timothy K. Earle, pp. 64–75. Cambridge University Press, Cambridge.

Eastman, Jane M.

2001   Life Courses and Gender among Late Prehistoric Siouan Communities. In *Archaeological Studies of Gender in the Southeastern United States,* edited by Jane M. Eastman and Christopher B. Rodning, pp. 57–76. University Press of Florida, Gainesville.

Edwards, J. Kenneth, R. Larry Marchinton, and Gladys F. Smith

1982   Pelvic Girdle Criteria for Sex Determination of White-Tailed Deer. *Journal of Wildlife Management* 46(2):544–547.

Egloff, Keith T.

1987   *Ceramic Study of Woodland Occupation along the Clinch and Powell Rivers in Southwest Virginia.* Virginia Department of Historic Resources, Richmond.

1992   The Late Woodland Period in Southwestern Virginia. In *Middle and*

Late Woodland Research in Virginia: A Synthesis, edited by Theodore R. Reinhart and Mary Ellen N. Hodges, pp. 187–223. Special Publication 29. Archeological Society of Virginia, Richmond.

Egloff, Keith, and Celia Reed

    1980   Crab Orchard Site: A Late Woodland Palisaded Village. *Archeological Society of Virginia Quarterly Bulletin* 34(3):130–148.

Egloff, Keith T., and E. Randolph Turner

    1988   Archaeological Investigations at the Richlands Hospital Site (44TZ51). *Archeological Society of Virginia Quarterly Bulletin* 43:14–23.

Elder, William H.

    1965   Primeval Deer Hunting Pressures Revealed by Remains from American Indian Middens. *Journal of Wildlife Management* 29(2):366–370.

Emerson, Thomas E.

    1980   A Stable White-Tailed Deer Population Model and Its Implications for Interpreting Prehistoric Hunting Patterns. *Mid-Continental Journal of Archaeology* 5(1):117–132.

Ernst, Carl H., Roger W. Barbour, and Jeffrey E. Lovich

    1994   *Turtles of the United States and Canada.* Smithsonian Institution Press, Washington, D.C.

Ewan, Joseph, and Nesta Ewan (editors)

    1970   *John Banister and His Natural History of Virginia, 1678–1692.* University of Illinois Press, Urbana.

Ewers, John C.

    1945   *Blackfeet Crafts.* Education Division, United States Indian Service, Lawrence, Kansas.

Fausz, J. Frederick

    1983   Profits, Pelts, and Power: English Culture in the Early Chesapeake, 1620–1652. *Maryland Historian* 14:15–30.

    1985   Patterns of Anglo-Indian Aggression and Accommodation along the Mid-Atlantic Coast, 1584–1634. In *Cultures in Contact: The European Impact on Native Cultural Institutions in Eastern North America, A.D. 1000–1800,* edited by William W. Fitzhugh, pp. 225–268. Smithsonian Institution Press, Washington, D.C.

Fitzhugh, William W.

    1985   *Cultures in Contact: The Impact of European Contacts on Native American Cultural Institutions, A.D. 1000–1800.* Smithsonian Institution Press, Washington, D.C.

Frank, Norman, and Erica Ramus

    1995   *A Complete Guide to Scientific and Common Names of Reptiles and Amphibians of the World.* N. G. Publishing, Inc., Pottsville, Pennsylvania.

Frison, George

    1970   The Glenrock Buffalo Jump, 48Co304: Late Prehistoric Period Buffalo Procurement and Butchering on the Northwestern Plains. Memoir No. 7. *Plains Anthropologist* 15(50/2):1–66.

Gallay, Alan

    2002   *The Indian Slave Trade: The Rise of the English Empire in the American South, 1670–1717.* Yale University Press, New Haven

Gallivan, Martin D.

    2003   *James River Chiefdoms: The Rise of Social Inequality in the Chesapeake.* University of Nebraska Press, Lincoln.

Gardner, William M.

    1979   Phase I Archaeological Resources Reconnaissance of the Proposed Appalachian Power Company Hydroelectric Project in Poor Valley and Hidden Valley, Washington County, Virginia. Thunderbird Research Corporation, Woodstock, Virginia.

Geier, Clarence R.

    1983   The Continuum of Late Woodland/Protohistoric Settlement along a Section of the Jackson River in the Ridge and Valley Province of Virginia: An Initial Formulation. *Archeological Society of Virginia Quarterly Bulletin* 38(4):234–276.

Geier, Clarence R., and Melissa McFee

    1981   *The Harry Jaeger Site (44BA489): A Multicomponent Protohistoric Indian/ Eighteenth Century Historic Site, Bath County, Virginia.* Occasional Papers in Anthropology No. 7. Archaeological Research Center, James Madison University, Harrisonburg.

Geier, Clarence R., and J. Craig Warren

    1982   *The Noah's Ark Site (44BA15): A Late Woodland/Protohistoric Site on the Jackson River, Bath County, Virginia.* Occasional Papers in Anthropology No. 14. Archaeological Research Center, James Madison University, Harrisonburg.

Gentry, Anthea, Juliet Clutton-Brock, and Colin P. Graves

    1996   Proposed Conservation of Usage of 15 Mammal Specific Names Based on Wild Species Which Are Antedated by or Contemporary with Those Based on Domestic Animals. *Bulletin of Zoological Nomenclature* 53(1): 28–37.

    2004   The Naming of Wild Animal Species and Their Domestic Derivatives. *Journal of Archaeological Science* 31:645–651.

Gifford, Diane P.

    1981   Taphonomy and Paleoecology: A Critical Review of Archaeology's Sister Disciplines. In *Advances in Archaeological Method and Theory*, Vol. 4, edited by Michael B. Schiffer, pp. 365–438. Academic Press, New York.

Gleach, Frederic W.

    1997   *Powhatan's World and Colonial Virginia: A Conflict of Cultures.* University of Nebraska Press, Lincoln.

Gold, Debra L.
1999   Subsistence, Health, and Emergent Inequality in Late Prehistoric Interior Virginia. Ph.D. dissertation, Department of Anthropology, University of Michigan, Ann Arbor.

Good, Mary Elizabeth
1972   *Guebert Site: An 18th Century Historic Kaskaskia Indian Village in Randolph County, Illinois.* Memoir No. 2, Central States Archaeological Societies, Inc., St. Louis.

Grayson, Donald K.
1978   Minimum Numbers and Sample Size in Vertebrate Faunal Analysis. *American Antiquity* 43(1):53–65.

1979   On the Quantification of Vertebrate Archaeofaunas. In *Advances in Archaeological Method and Theory,* Vol. 2, edited by Michael B. Schiffer, pp. 199–237. Academic Press, New York.

1984   *Quantitative Zooarchaeology: Topics in the Analysis of Archaeological Faunas.* Academic Press, New York.

Gregory, Christopher A.
1982   *Gifts and Commodities.* Academic Press, New York.

Gremillion, Kristen J.
1987   Plant Remains from the Fredericks, Wall, and Mitchum Sites. In *The Siouan Project: Seasons I and II,* edited by Roy S. Dickens, Jr., H. Trawick Ward, and R. P. Stephen Davis, Jr., pp. 259–277. Monograph Series No. 1. Research Laboratories of Anthropology, University of North Carolina, Chapel Hill.

1993a   Archaeobotany of the Graham-White Site. Report on file with the Virginia Department of Historic Resources, Richmond.

1993b   Adoption of Old World Crops and Processes of Cultural Change in the Historical Southeast. *Southeastern Archaeology* 12(1):15–20.

Guilday, John E.
1971   *Biological and Archeological Analysis of Bones from a 17th Century Indian Village (46PU31), Putnam County, West Virginia.* Report of Archaeological Investigations No. 4. West Virginia Geological and Economic Survey, Morgantown.

Guilday, John E., Paul W. Parmalee, and Donald P. Tanner
1962   Aboriginal Butchering Techniques at the Eschelman Site (36LA12), Lancaster County, Pennsylvania. *Pennsylvania Archaeologist* 32:59–83.

Halls, Lowell K. (editor)
1984   *White-Tailed Deer: Ecology and Management.* Stackpole Books, Harrisburg, Pennsylvania.

Hamell, George R.
1983   Trading in Metaphors: The Magic of Beads. In *Proceedings of the 1982 Glass Trade Bead Conference,* edited by Charles F. Hayes III pp. 5–28.

Research Records No. 16. Rochester Museum and Science Center, Rochester.

Hamlin, Kenneth L., David F. Pac, Carolyn A. Sime, Richard M. DeSimone, and Gary L. Dusek

2000   Evaluating the Accuracy of Ages Obtained by Two Methods for Montana Ungulates. *Journal of Wildlife Management* 64(2):441–449.

Hammett, Julia E.

1987   Shell Artifacts from the Carolina Piedmont. In *The Siouan Project: Seasons I and II,* edited by Roy S. Dickens, Jr., H. Trawick Ward, and R. P. Stephen Davis, Jr., pp. 167–183. Monograph Series No. 1. Research Laboratories of Anthropology, University of North Carolina, Chapel Hill.

Hammett, Julia E., and Beverly A. Sizemore

1989   Shell Beads and Ornaments: Socioeconomic Indicators of the Past. In *Proceedings of the 1986 Shell Bead Conference,* edited by Charles F. Hayes III pp. 125–137. Research Records No. 20. Rochester Museum and Science Center, Rochester, New York.

Hantman, Jeffrey L.

1990   Between Powhatan and Quirank: Reconstructing Monacan Culture and History in the Context of Jamestown. *American Anthropologist* 92: 676–690.

1993   Powhatan's Relations with the Piedmont Monacans. In *Powhatan Foreign Relations,* edited by Helen Rountree, pp. 94–111. University of Virginia Press, Charlottesville.

2001   Monacan Archaeology of the Virginia Interior, A.D. 1400–1700. In *Societies in Eclipse: Archaeology of the Eastern Woodlands Indians, A.D. 1400–1700,* edited by David S. Brose, C. Wesley Cowan, and Robert C. Mainfort, Jr., pp. 107–123. Smithsonian Institution Press, Washington, D.C.

Hantman, Jeffrey L., and Debra L. Gold

2002   The Woodland in the Middle Atlantic: Ranking and Dynamic Political Stability. In *The Woodland Southeast,* edited by David G. Anderson and Robert C. Mainfort, Jr., pp. 270–291. University of Alabama Press, Tuscaloosa.

Harris, R. K., and Inus Marie Harris

1967   Trade Beads, Projectile Points, and Knives. In *A Pilot Study: Wichita Indian Archaeology and Ethnohistory,* edited by Robert E. Bell, Edward B. Jelks, and W. W. Newcomb, pp. 129–161. Final Report for Grant GS-964. National Science Foundation, Washington, D.C.

Hatley, M. Thomas

1989   The Three Lives of Keowee: Loss and Recovery in Eighteenth-Century Cherokee Villages. In *Powhatan's Mantle: Indians in the Colonial Southeast,* edited by Peter H. Wood, Gregory A. Waselkov, and M. Thomas Hatley, pp. 223–248. University of Nebraska Press, Lincoln.

Heidenreich, Conrad E., and Arthur J. Ray
   1976   *The Early Fur Trades: A Study in Cultural Interaction.* McClelland and Stewart, Toronto.

Henning, William W.
   1823a   *The Statutes at Large; Being a Collection of All the Laws of Virginia, From the First Session of the Legislature, in the Year 1619,* Vol. 1 (1619–1660). Commonwealth of Virginia, Richmond.
   1823b   *The Statutes at Large; Being a Collection of All the Laws of Virginia, From the First Session of the Legislature, in the Year 1619,* Vol. 2 (1660–1682). Commonwealth of Virginia, Richmond.
   1823c   *The Statutes at Large; Being a Collection of All the Laws of Virginia, From the First Session of the Legislature, in the Year 1619,* Vol. 3 (1683–1710). Commonwealth of Virginia, Richmond.

Hickerson, Daniel A.
   1996   Trade, Mediation, and Political Status in the Hasinai Confederacy. *Research in Economic Anthropology* 17:149–168.

Hiller, Ilo
   1996   *The White-Tailed Deer.* Texas A&M University Press, College Station.

Holland, C. G.
   1970   *An Archeological Survey of Southwest Virginia.* Smithsonian Institution Press, Washington, D.C.

Holm, Mary Ann
   1987   Faunal Remains from the Wall and Fredericks Sites. In *The Siouan Project: Seasons I and II,* edited by Roy S. Dickens, Jr., H. Trawick Ward, and R. P. Stephen Davis, Jr., pp. 237–258. Monograph Series No. 1. Research Laboratories of Anthropology, University of North Carolina, Chapel Hill.

Hudson, Charles M., Jr.
   1976   *The Southeastern Indians.* University of Tennessee Press, Knoxville.
   1981   Why the Southeastern Indians Slaughtered Deer. In *Indians, Animals, and the Fur Trade: A Critique of Keepers of the Game,* edited by Shepard Krech III pp. 156–176. University of Georgia Press, Athens.
   1990   *The Juan Pardo Expedition: Explorations of the Carolinas and Tennessee, 1566–1568.* Smithsonian Institution Press, Washington, D.C.

Hudson, Charles M., Jr., and Carmen Chaves Tesser (editors)
   1994   *The Forgotten Centuries: Indians and Europeans in the American South, 1521–1704.* University of Georgia Press, Athens.

Hulton, Paul
   1984   *America 1585: The Complete Drawings of John White.* University of North Carolina Press, Chapel Hill.

Hutchinson, Dale L., and Lorraine V. Aragon
   2002   Collective Burials and Community Memories: Interpreting the Place-

ment of the Dead in the Southeastern and Mid-Atlantic United States with Reference to Ethnographic Cases from Indonesia. In *The Space and Place of Death,* edited by Helaine Silverman and David B. Small, pp. 27–54. Archaeological Papers No. 11. American Anthropological Association, Arlington, Virginia.

Hutchinson, Dale L., Clark Spencer Larsen, Margaret J. Schoeninger, and Lynette Norr

    1998   Regional Variation in the Pattern of Maize Adoption and Use in Florida and Georgia. *American Antiquity* 63(3):397–416.

Innis, Harold A.

    1962   *The Fur Trade in Canada.* Yale University Press, New Haven.

International Council of Tanners

    1975   *International Glossary of Leather Terms.* 2nd ed. International Council of Tanners, London.

Jackson, H. Edwin

    1989   The Trouble with Transformations: Effects of Sample Size and Sample Composition on Meat Weight Estimates Based on Skeletal Mass Allometry. *Journal of Archaeological Science* 16:601–610.

James, Steven R.

    1997   Methodological Issues Concerning Screen Size Recovery Rates and Their Effects on Archaeofaunal Interpretations. *Journal of Archaeological Science* 24:385–397.

Jefferies, Richard W.

    2001   Living on the Edge: Mississippian Settlement in the Cumberland Gap Vicinity. In *Archaeology of the Appalachian Highlands,* edited by Lynne P. Sullivan and Susan C. Prezzano, pp. 198–221. University of Tennessee Press, Knoxville.

Jenkins, Robert E., and Noel M. Burkhead

    1994   *Freshwater Fishes of Virginia.* American Fisheries Society, Bethesda, Maryland.

Johnson, Larry Dean

    1982   The Huffman Site, Bath County, Virginia. In *Prehistory of the Gathright Dam Area, Virginia,* edited by Howard A. MacCord, Sr., pp. 29–45. Richmond.

Johnson, William C., and William P. Athens

    1998   Late Prehistoric Period Monongahela Culture Settlement Patterns in the Appalachian Plateaus Section of the Upper Ohio River Valley: The Case for a Risk Reduction Subsistence Strategy. Paper presented at the Pennsylvania Archaeological Council Meeting, New Cumberland.

Jones, Emory E.

    n.d.   A Preliminary Report: The Hoge Site (44TZ6), Burkes Garden, Virginia. Report on file with the Virginia Department of Historic Resources, Richmond.

Jones, Emory E., and Howard A. MacCord, Sr.

    2001   The Hoge Site, Tazewell County, Virginia. In *Contributions to the Ar-chaeology of Southwestern Virginia: A Volume Honoring the Author Emory Eugene Jones, Jr., of Bluefield, West Virginia,* pp. 109–182. Special Publication No. 40. Archeological Society of Virginia, Richmond.

Judd, Carol M., and Arthur J. Ray (editors)

    1980   *Old Trails and New Directions: Papers of the Third North American Fur Trade Conference.* University of Toronto Press, Toronto.

Kellogg, Remington

    1956   What and Where Are Whitetails. In *The Deer of North America: Their History and Management,* edited by Walter P. Taylor, pp. 31–55. Stackpole Company, Harrisburg, Pennsylvania; The Wildlife Management Institute, Washington, D.C.

Kelso, William M.

    1995   *Jamestown Rediscovery I: Search For 1607 James Fort.* The Association for the Preservation of Virginia Antiquities, Jamestown, Virginia.

Kent, Barry C.

    1984   *Susquehanna's Indians.* Anthropological Series No. 6. Pennsylvania Historical and Museum Commission, Commonwealth of Pennsylvania, Harrisburg.

Kidd, Kenneth E., and Martha A. Kidd

    1970   A Classification System for Glass Beads for the Use of Field Archaeologists. Canadian Historic Sites: Occasional Papers in Archaeology and History 1, Parks Canada, Ottawa. Reprinted in *Proceedings of the 1982 Glass Bead Conference,* edited by Charles F. Hayes III. Research Records 16, Rochester Museum and Science Division, Rochester, Appendix, 1983.

Kidwell, Clara Sue

    1995   Choctaw Women and Cultural Persistence in Mississippi. In *Negotiators of Change: Historical Perspectives on Native American Women,* edited by Nancy Shoemaker, pp. 115–134. Routledge, New York.

Klatka, Thomas S., and Michael J. Klein

    1998   Deciphering the Site Occupational History at the Graham-White Site (44RN21). *Journal of Middle Atlantic Archaeology* 14:127–145.

Klein, Michael J., Kate Martin, and Josh Duncan

    2003   Analysis of Ceramics from Selected Contexts at the Trigg Site (44MY3). Report on file with the Virginia Department of Historic Resources, Richmond.

Klein, Laura F., and Lillian A. Ackerman

    1995   *Women and Power in Native North America.* University of Oklahoma Press, Norman.

Klein, Richard G.

    1979   Stone Age Exploitation of Animals in Southern Africa. *American Scientist* 67:150–160.

Klein, Richard, and Kathryn Cruz-Uribe
    1984   *The Analysis of Animal Bones from Archaeological Sites.* University of Chicago Press, Chicago.

Knox, W. Matt
    1996   1995 Virginia Deer Harvest Summary. *Wildlife Resource Bulletin* 96(4):1–17.
    1997   Historical Changes in the Abundance and Distribution of Deer in Virginia. In *The Science of Overabundance: Deer Ecology and Population Management,* edited by William J. McShea, H. Brian Underwood, and John H. Rappole, pp. 27–36. Smithsonian Institution Press, Washington, D.C.

Kraft, Herbert C.
    1972   The Miller Field Site, Warren County, New Jersey. In *Archaeology in the Upper Delaware Valley: A Study of the Cultural Chronology of the Tocks Islands Reservoir,* edited by W. Fred Kinsey. III, pp. 1–54. Anthropological Series No. 2. Pennsylvania Historical and Museum Commission, Commonwealth of Pennsylvania, Harrisburg.

Landon, David
    1993   Testing Seasonal Slaughter Model for Colonial New England Using Tooth Cementum Increment Analysis. *Journal of Archaeological Science* 20:439–455.

Lapham, Heather A.
    1998   Vertebrate Fauna from the Thomas Wharf Site (44NH1), Nassawadox, Virginia. Report on file with The Center for Archaeological Research, College of William and Mary, Williamsburg, Virginia.
    2000   Vertebrate Fauna from 31WL37, Wilson County, North Carolina. Report on file with TRC Garrow Associates, Inc., Chapel Hill, North Carolina.
    2002   *Deerskin Production and Prestige Goods Acquisition in Late Woodland and Early Historic Southwest Virginia.* Ph.D. dissertation. University Microfilms International, Ann Arbor.

Larsen, Clark Spencer, Dale L. Hutchinson, Margaret J. Schoeninger, and Lynette Norr
    2001   Food and Stable Isotopes in La Florida: Diet and Nutrition before and after Contact. In *Bioarchaeology of Spanish Florida: The Impact of Colonialism,* edited by Clark Spencer Larsen, pp. 52–81. University Press of Florida, Gainesville.

Leacock, Eleanor
    1978   Women's Status in Egalitarian Society: Implications for Social Evolution. *Current Anthropology* 19(2):247–275.

Lederer, John
    1966   *The Discoveries of John Lederer, In Three Several Marches from Virginia, To the West of Carolina, and Other Parts of the Continent: Begun in March 1669, and Ended in September 1670.* March of America Facsimile Series No. 25. University Microfilms, Ann Arbor.

Lefler, Hugh T. (editor)
  1967   *A New Voyage to Carolina by John Lawson.* University of North Carolina Press, Chapel Hill.

Lewis, Oscar
  1942   *The Effects of White Contact upon Blackfoot Culture, with Special Reference to the Role of the Fur Trade.* Monographs of the American Ethnological Society No. 6. J. J. Augustin Publishers, New York.

Lieberman, Daniel
  1994   The Biological Basis for Seasonal Increments in Dental Cementum and Their Application to Archaeological Research. *Journal of Archaeological Science* 21:525–539.

Lightfoot, Kent G.
  1995   Culture Contact Studies: Redefining the Relationship between Prehistoric and Historical Archaeology. *American Antiquity* 60(2):199–217.

Lightfoot, Kent G., and Gary M. Feinman
  1982   Social Differentiation and Leadership Development in Early Pithouse Villages in the Mogollon Region of the American Southwest. *American Antiquity* 47(1):64–86.

Linnaeus, Carolus
  1758   *Systema Naturae.* 10th ed., reformata. Laurentii Salvii, Stockholm.

Linzey, Donald W.
  1998   *The Mammals of Virginia.* McDonald and Woodward Publishing, Blacksburg, Virginia.

Lyman, R. Lee
  1987a   Zooarchaeology and Taphonomy: A General Consideration. *Journal of Ethnobiology* 7(1):93–117.
  1987b   On the Analysis of Vertebrate Mortality Profiles: Sample Size, Mortality Type, and Hunting Pressure. *American Antiquity* 52(1):125–142.
  1987c   Archaeofaunas and Butchery Studies: A Taphonomic Perspective. In *Advances in Archaeological Method and Theory,* Vol. 10, edited by Michael B. Schiffer, pp. 249–337. Academic Press, New York.
  1994a   Quantitative Units and Terminology in Zooarchaeology. *American Antiquity* 59(1):36–71.
  1994b   *Vertebrate Taphonomy.* Cambridge University Press, Cambridge.

MacCord, Howard A., Sr.
  1977   Trade Goods from the Trigg Site, Radford, Virginia. In *The Conference on Historic Site Archaeology Papers 10,* edited by Stanley A. South, pp. 60–68. University of South Carolina Press, Columbia.
  1984   The Trigg Site, Radford, Virginia: A Resume. In *Upland Archeology in the East: Symposium 2,* edited by Michael B. Barber, pp. 178–179. Cultural Resources Report No. 5, Forest Service Southern Region. United States Department of Agriculture, Atlanta, Georgia.

1989a The Intermontane Culture: A Middle Appalachian Late Woodland Manifestation. *Archaeology of Eastern North America* 17:89–108.

1989b The Contact Period in Virginia. *Journal of Middle Atlantic Archaeology* 5:121–128.

MacCord, Howard A., Sr. (editor)

1986 *The Lewis Creek Mound Culture in Virginia.* Privately printed, Richmond.

MacCord, Howard A., Sr., and William T. Buchanan, Jr.

1980 *The Crab Orchard Site, Tazewell County, Virginia.* Archeological Society of Virginia, Richmond.

Mallios, Seth W.

1998 In the Hands of "Indian Givers": Exchange and Violence at Ajacan, Roanoke, and Jamestown. Ph.D. dissertation, Department of Anthropology, University of Virginia, Charlottesville.

Martin, Calvin

1978 *Keepers of the Game: Indian-Animal Relationships and the Fur Trade.* University of California Press, Berkeley.

Martin, Joel W.

1994 Southeastern Indians and the English Trade in Skins and Slaves. In *The Forgotten Centuries: Indians and Europeans in the American South, 1521–1704,* edited by Charles Hudson and Carmen Chaves Tesser, pp. 304–324. University of Georgia Press, Athens.

Mauss, Marcel

1925 *The Gift: The Form and Reason for Exchange in Archaic Societies.* W. W. Norton, New York (1990).

Mayer-Oakes, William J.

1955 *Prehistory of the Upper Ohio Valley: An Introductory Archaeological Study.* Anthropological Series No. 2, Annals. Carnegie Museum, Pittsburgh.

McCabe, Thomas R., and Richard E. McCabe

1997 Recounting Whitetails Past. In *The Science of Overabundance: Deer Ecology and Population Management,* edited by William J. McShea, H. Brian Underwood, and John H. Rappole, pp. 11–26. Smithsonian Institution Press, Washington, D.C.

McCullough, Dale R.

1979 *The George Reserve Deer Herd: Population Ecology of K-Selected Species.* University of Michigan Press, Ann Arbor.

McDonald, Jerry N.

1984 Population Analysis of the Trigg Site White Tail Deer. In *The Trigg Site, City of Radford, Virginia,* by William T. Buchanan, pp. 459–476. Appendix D. Archeological Society of Virginia, Richmond.

McDowell, William L., Jr. (editor)

1955 *Journals of the Commissioners of the Indian Trade, September 20, 1710–*

August 29, 1718. Colonial Records of South Carolina, South Carolina Archives Department, Columbia.

McGinnes, Burd S., and Robert L. Downing

1973   Variation in Peaks of Fawning in Virginia. In *Proceedings of the Twenty-Sixth Annual Conference,* edited by Arnold. L. Mitchell, pp. 22–27. Southeastern Association of Game and Fish Commissioners, Columbia, South Carolina.

McGinnes, Burd S., and John H. Reeves, Jr.

1957   A Comparison of Pre-Historic Indian Killed Deer to the Modern Deer. *Archeological Society of Virginia Quarterly Bulletin* 12(1):5–8.

McIlhany, Calvert W.

1986   Archaeological Survey and Testing at the Tazewell County Historical Park and the Crab Orchard Site (44TZ1) in Tazewell County, Virginia. Report on file with the Virginia Department of Historic Resources, Richmond.

McKenna, Malcolm C., and Susan K. Bell

1997   *Classification of Mammals above the Species Level.* Columbia University Press, New York.

Merrell, James

1989   *The Indians' New World: Catawbas and Their Neighbors from European Contact through the Era of Removal.* University of North Carolina Press, Chapel Hill.

Metcalf, Peter, and Richard Huntington

1991   *Celebrations of Death: The Anthropology of Mortuary Ritual.* 2nd ed. Cambridge University Press, Cambridge.

Meyers, Maureen S.

2002   The Mississippian Frontier in Southwestern Virginia. *Southeastern Archaeology* 21(2):178–191.

Milanich, Jerald T.

1994   Franciscan Missions and Native Peoples in Spanish Florida. In *The Forgotten Centuries: Indians and Europeans in the American South, 1521–1704,* edited by Charles Hudson and Carmen Chaves Tesser, pp. 276–303. University of Georgia Press, Athens.

1999   *Laboring in the Fields of the Lord: Spanish Missions and Southeastern Indians.* Smithsonian Institution Press, Washington, D.C.

Miller, Christopher L, and George R. Hamell

1986   A New Perspective on Indian-White Contact: Cultural Symbols and Colonial Trade. *Journal of American History* 73(2):311–328.

Mitchell, Joseph C.

1994   *The Reptiles of Virginia.* Smithsonian Institution Press, Washington, D.C.

Moore, Elizabeth A., and Heather A. Lapham

1997   Vertebrate Fauna from the Graham-White Site, 44RN21. Report on file with the Roanoke Regional Preservation Office, Virginia Department of Historic Resources.

Morey, Darcy F.

1986   Studies on Amerindian Dogs: Taxonomic Analysis of Canid Crania from the Northern Plains. *Journal of Archaeological Science* 13:119–145.

1994   The Early Evolution of the Domestic Dog. *American Scientist* 82(4): 336–347.

Munson, Patrick J.

1991   Mortality Profiles of White-Tailed Deer from Archaeological Sites in Eastern North America: Selective Hunting or Taphonomy? In *Beamers, Bobwhites, and Blue-Points: Tributes to the Career of Paul W. Parmalee*, edited by James R. Purdue, Walter E. Klippel, and Bonnie W. Styles, pp. 139–151. Scientific Papers No. 23. Illinois State Museum, Springfield.

Munson, Patrick J., and Rexford C. Garniewicz

2002   Age-Mediated Survivorship of Ungulate Mandibles and Teeth in Canid-Ravaged Faunal Assemblages. *Journal of Archaeological Science* 30:405–416.

Nassaney, Michael S.

2000   Archaeology and Oral Tradition in Tandem: Interpreting Native American Ritual, Ideology, and Gender Relations in Contact-Period Southeastern New England. In *Interpretations of Native North American Life: Materials Contributions to Ethnohistory,* edited by Michael S. Nassaney and Eric S. Johnson, pp. 412–431. University Press of Florida, Gainesville.

Nelson, Joseph S.

1994   *Fishes of the World.* 3rd ed. J. Wiley, New York.

Nickerson, Max Allen, and Charles Edwin Mays

1973   *The Hellbenders: North American "Giant Salamanders."* Publications in Biology and Geology No. 1. Milwaukee Public Museum, Milwaukee.

Norr, Lynette

1995   Interpreting Dietary Maize from Bone Stable Isotopes in the American Tropics: The State of the Art. In *Archaeology in the Lowland American Tropics: Current Analytical Methods and Applications,* edited by Peter W. Stahl, pp. 198–223. Cambridge University Press, Cambridge.

2002   Stable Isotope Analysis and Dietary Inference. In *Foraging, Farming, and Coastal Biocultural Adaptation in Late Prehistoric North Carolina,* by Dale L. Hutchinson, pp. 178–205. Appendix B. University Press of Florida, Gainesville.

Olsen, Stanley J.

1985   *Origins of the Domestic Dog: The Fossil Record.* University of Arizona Press, Tucson.

O'Shea, John M.

1996   *Villagers of the Marcos: A Portrait of an Early Bronze Age Society.* Plenum Press, New York.

Owsley, Douglas W.

1992 Demography of Prehistoric and Early Historic Northern Plains Popula-
tions. In *Disease and Demography in the Americas,* edited by John W.
Verano and Douglas H. Ubelaker, pp. 75–86. Smithsonian Institution
Press, Washington, D.C.

Ozoga, John L., and Louis J. Verme

1982 Physical and Reproductive Characteristics of a Supplementally Fed
White-Tailed Deer Herd. *Journal of Wildlife Management* 46(2):281–301.

Parker Pearson, Michael

1984 Economic and Ideological Change: Cyclical Growth in Pre-State Societies of Jutland. In *Ideology, Power and Prehistory,* edited by Daniel Miller
and Christopher Tilley, pp. 69–92. Cambridge University Press, Cambridge.

Parmalee, Paul W., and Arthur E. Bogan

1998 *The Freshwater Mussels of Tennessee.* University of Tennessee Press, Knoxville.

Parrish, Shirley Virginia

1972 The Fur and Skin Trade of Colonial Virginia. Master's thesis, Department of History, Old Dominion University, Norfolk, Virginia.

Pavao-Zuckerman, Barnet

2000 Vertebrate Subsistence in the Mississippian-Historic Transition. *Southeastern Archaeology* 19(2):135–144.

Payne, Sebastian

1972 Partial Recovery and Sample Bias: The Results of Some Sieving Experi-
ments. In *Papers in Economic Prehistory,* edited by E. S. Higgs, pp. 49–
64. Cambridge University Press, Cambridge.

1975 Partial Recovery and Sample Bias. In *Archaeozoological Studies,* edited by
A. T. Clason, pp. 7–17. North-Holland Publishing, Amsterdam.

Peake, Ora Brooks

1954 *A History of the United States Indian Factory System, 1795–1822.* Sage
Books, Denver.

Peebles, Christopher S., and Susan M. Kus

1977 Some Archaeological Correlates of Ranked Societies. *American Antiquity*
42:421–448.

Perdue, Theda

1998 *Cherokee Women: Gender and Culture Change, 1700–1835.* University of
Nebraska Press, Lincoln.

Perry, Richard J.

1979 The Fur Trade and the Status of Women in the Western Subarctic. *Ethnohistory* 26(4):363–375.

Petherick, Gary L.

1987 Architecture and Features at the Fredericks, Wall, and Mitchum Sites.

In *The Siouan Project: Seasons I and II,* edited by Roy S. Dickens, Jr., H. Trawick Ward, and R. P. Stephen Davis, Jr., pp. 29–80. Monograph Series No. 1. Research Laboratories of Anthropology, University of North Carolina, Chapel Hill.

Phillips, Paul

1961   *The Fur Trade.* University of Oklahoma Press, Norman.

Polhemus, Richard R. (editor)

1987   *The Toqua Site (40MR6): A Late Mississippian, Dallas Phase Town.* Report of Investigations No. 41. Department of Anthropology, University of Tennessee, Knoxville; Publications in Anthropology No. 44. Tennessee Valley Authority.

Potter, Stephen R.

1989   Early English Effects on Virginia Algonquian Exchange and Tribute in the Tidewater Potomac. In *Powhatan's Mantle: Indians in the Colonial Southeast,* edited by Peter H. Wood, Gregory A. Waselkov, and M. Thomas Hatley, pp. 151–172. University of Nebraska Press, Lincoln.

1993   *Commoners, Tribute, and Chiefs: The Development of Algonquian Culture in the Potomac Valley.* University of Virginia Press, Charlottesville.

Purdue, James R.

1986   The Size of White-Tailed Deer (*Odocoileus virginianus*) during the Archaic Period in Central Illinois. In *Foraging, Collecting, and Harvesting: Archaic Period Subsistence and Settlement in the Eastern Woodlands,* edited by Sarah W. Neusius, pp. 65–95. Occasional Papers No. 6. Center for Archaeological Investigations, Southern Illinois University, Carbondale.

Quinn, David B., and Alison M. Quinn (editors)

1973   *Virginia Voyages from Hakluyt.* Oxford University Press, London.

Reher, Charles A.

1974   Population Study of the Casper Site Bison. In *The Casper Site: A Hell Gap Bison Kill on the High Plains,* edited by George C. Frison, pp. 113–124. Academic Press, New York.

Reitz, Elizabeth J.

1991   Animal Use and Culture Change in Spanish Florida. In *Animal Use and Culture Change,* edited by Pam J. Crabtree and Kathleen Ryan, pp. 63–77. MASCA Research Papers in Science and Archaeology No. 8 Supplement. University Museum of Archaeology and Anthropology, University of Pennsylvania, Philadelphia.

Reitz, Elizabeth J., and Dan Cordier

1983   Use of Allometry in Zooarchaeological Analysis. In *Animals and Archaeology 2: Shell Middens, Fishes, and Birds,* edited by Juliet Clutton-Brock and Caroline Grigson, pp. 237–252. British Archaeological Reports International Series No. 183. Archaeopress, Oxford.

Reitz, Elizabeth J., Irvy R. Quitmyer, H. Stephen Hale, Sylvia J. Schudder, and
Elizabeth S. Wing
   1987   Application of Allometry to Zooarchaeology. *American Antiquity* 52(2):
               304–317.
Reitz, Elizabeth J., and Elizabeth S. Wing
   1999   *Zooarchaeology.* Cambridge University Press, Cambridge.
Ringrose, T. J.
   1993   Bone Counts and Statistics: A Critique. *Journal of Archaeological Science*
               20:121–157.
Robinson, W. Stitt
   1979   *The Southern Colonial Frontier, 1607–1763.* University of New Mexico
               Press, Albuquerque.
Rodning, Christopher B.
   2001   Mortuary Ritual and Gender Ideology in Protohistoric Southwestern
               North Carolina. In *Archaeological Studies of Gender in the Southeastern
               United States,* edited by Jane M. Eastman and Christopher B. Rodning,
               pp. 77–100. University Press of Florida, Gainesville.
Rogers, Daniel J.
   1990   *Objects of Change: The Archaeology and History of Arikara Contact with
               Europeans.* Smithsonian Institution Press, Washington, D.C.
Rogers, Daniel J., and Samuel M. Wilson
   1993   *Ethnohistory and Archaeology: Approaches to Postcontact Change in the
               Americas.* Plenum Press, New York.
Rountree, Helen C.
   1989   *The Powhatan Indians of Virginia.* University of Oklahoma Press, Norman.
   1998   Powhatan Indian Women: The People Captain John Smith Barely Saw.
               Ethnohistory 41(1):1–29.
Rountree, Helen C., and Thomas E. Davidson
   1997   *Eastern Shore Indians of Virginia and Maryland.* University Press of Vir-
               ginia, Charlottesville.
Rue, Leonard Lee
   1962   *The World of the White-Tailed Deer.* J. B. Lippincott, New York.
   1978   *The Deer of North America.* Crown, New York.
Sahlins, Marshall
   1972   *Stone Age Economics.* Aldine, Chicago.
   1985   *Islands of History.* University of Chicago Press, Chicago.
Sauer, Peggy R.
   1984   Physical Characteristics. In *White-Tailed Deer: Ecology and Management,*
               edited by Lowell K. Halls, pp. 73–90. Stackpole Books, Harrisburg,
               Pennsylvania.
Scarry, John F.
   1999   Elite Identities in the Apalachee Province: The Construction of Identity

and Cultural Change in a Mississippian Polity. In *Material Symbols: Culture and Economy in Prehistory,* edited by John E. Robb, pp. 342–361. Occasional Paper No. 26. Center for Archaeological Investigations, Southern Illinois University, Carbondale.

Schmidt-Nielsen, Knut

1984   *Scaling: Why Is Animal Size So Important?* Cambridge University Press, Cambridge.

Schroedl, Gerald F. (editor)

1986   *Overhill Cherokee Archaeology at Chota-Tanasee.* Report of Investigations 38. Department of Anthropology, University of Tennessee, Knoxville; Publications in Anthropology 42. Tennessee Valley Authority.

Schroedl, Gerald F., C. Clifford Boyd, Jr., and R. P. Stephen Davis, Jr.

1990   Explaining Mississippian Origins in East Tennessee. In *The Mississippian Emergence,* edited by Bruce D. Smith, pp. 175–196. Smithsonian Institution Press, Washington, D.C.

Schroedl, Gerald F., and Emanuel Breitburg

1986   Burials. In *Overhill Cherokee Archaeology at Chota-Tanasee,* edited by Gerald F. Schroedl, pp. 125–216. Report of Investigations 38. Department of Anthropology, University of Tennessee, Knoxville; Publications in Anthropology 42. Tennessee Valley Authority.

Schultz, Jackson S.

1876   *The Leather Manufacture in the United States: A Dissertation on the Methods and Economies of Tanning.* Shoe and Leather Reporter Office, New York.

Scott, Gary T., and Richard R. Polhemus

1987   Mortuary Patterning. In *The Toqua Site (40MR6): A Late Mississippian, Dallas Phase Town,* edited by Richard R. Polhemus, pp. 378–430. Report of Investigations No. 41. Department of Anthropology, University of Tennessee, Knoxville; Publications in Anthropology No. 44. Tennessee Valley Authority.

Severinghaus, C. W.

1949a   The Liveweight-Dressed Weight and Liveweight-Edible Meat Relationship. *New York State Conservationist* 30(1):26.

1949b   Tooth Development and Wear as Criteria of Age in White-Tailed Deer. *Journal of Wildlife Management* 13(2):195–216.

Severinghaus, C. W., and E. L. Cheatum

1956   Life and Times of White-Tailed Deer. In *The Deer of North America: Their History and Management,* edited by Walter P. Taylor, pp. 57–186. Stackpole Company, Harrisburg, Pennsylvania; The Wildlife Management Institute, Washington, D.C.

Shaffer, Brian S.

1992   Quarter-Inch Screening: Understanding Biases in Recovery of Vertebrate Faunal Remains. *American Antiquity* 57(1):129–136.

Shennan, Stephen

   1982   Exchange and Ranking: The Role of Amber in the Earlier Bonze Age of
             Europe. In *Ranking, Resource, and Exchange,* edited by Colin Renfrew
             and Stephen Shennan, pp. 33–45. Cambridge University Press, Cam-
             bridge.

Sibley, Charles G., and Burt L. Monroe, Jr.

   1990   *Distribution and Taxonomy of Birds of the World.* Yale University Press,
             New Haven.

Sleeper-Smith, Susan

   2000   Women, Kin, and Catholicism: New Perspectives on the Fur Trade.
             Ethnohistory 47(2):423–452.

Smith, Bruce D.

   1974   Predator-Prey Relationships in the Southern Ozarks—A.D. 1300. *Hu-
             man Ecology* 1(2):31–43.

   1975   *Middle Mississippi Exploitation of Animal Populations.* Anthropological
             Papers No. 57. Museum of Anthropology, University of Michigan, Ann
             Arbor.

Smith, Marvin T.

   1987   *Archaeology of Aboriginal Culture Change in the Interior Southeast: De-
             population during the Early Historic Period.* University Press of Florida,
             Gainesville.

Speth, John D.

   1983   *Bison Kills and Bone Counts: Decision Making by Ancient Hunters.* Uni-
             versity of Chicago Press, Chicago.

Spiess, Arthur E.

   1990   Deer Tooth Sectioning, Eruption, and Seasonality of Deer Hunting in
             Prehistoric Maine. *Man in the Northeast* 39:29–44.

Stauffer, Jay R., Jr., Jeffrey M. Boltz, and Laura R. White

   1995   The Fishes of West Virginia. *Proceedings of the Academy of Natural Sci-
             ences of Philadelphia* 146:1–389.

Sternheimer, Patricia A.

   1983   Classification and Analysis of the Grave Goods from the Trigg Site: A
             Late Woodland–Contact Burial Site in Southwestern Virginia. Master's
             thesis, Department of Anthropology, University of Virginia, Charlottes-
             ville.

Stewart, R. Michael

   1989   Trade and Exchange in Middle Atlantic Region Prehistory. *Archaeology
             of Eastern North America* 17:47–88.

   1995   The Status of Woodland Prehistory in the Middle Atlantic Region. *Ar-
             chaeology of Eastern North America* 23:177–206.

Stine, Linda Frances

   1990   *Mercantilism and Piedmont Peltry: Colonial Perceptions of the Southern
             Fur Trade, Circa 1640–1740.* Volumes in Historical Archaeology No. 14.

South Carolina Institute of Archaeology and Anthropology, University of South Carolina, Columbia.

Stiner, Mary C. Steven L. Kuhn, Stephen Weiner, and Ofer Bar-Yosef
1995   Differential Burning, Recrystallization, and Fragmentation of Archaeological Bone. *Journal of Archaeological Science* 22:223–237.

Stone, Lyle M.
1974   *Fort Michilimackinac, 1715–1781: An Archaeological Perspective on the Revolutionary Frontier.* Anthropological Series. Publications of the Museum, Michigan State University, East Lansing.

Stubbs, Jane
1960   Virginia's Colonial Fur Trade. *Virginia Cavalcade* 10(3):41–47.

Stüwe, Michael
1986   Behavior and Ecology of a White-Tailed Deer Population (*Odocoileus virginianus*) at High Density. Ph.D. dissertation, Department of Biology, Bielefeld University, Bielefeld, Germany.

Swanton, John
1946   *The Indians of the Southeastern United States.* Bureau of American Ethnology Bulletin No. 137. Government Printing Office, Washington, D.C.

Tanners' Council of America
1946   *Dictionary of Leather Terminology.* 4th ed. Tanners' Council of America, New York.

Taylor, Walter P. (editor)
1956   *The Deer of North America: Their History and Management.* Stackpole Company, Harrisburg, Pennsylvania; The Wildlife Management Institute, Washington, D.C.

Thomas, Nicholas
1991   *Entangled Objects: Exchange, Material Culture, and Colonialism in the Pacific.* Harvard University Press, Cambridge.

Tinling, Marion (editor)
1977   *The Correspondence of the Three William Byrds of Westover, Virginia, 1684–1776.* University of Virginia Press, Charlottesville.

Trigger, Bruce G.
1976   *The Children of the Aataentsic: A History of the Huron People to 1660,* Vols. 1 and 2. McGill-Queen's University Press, Montreal.
1990   Maintaining Economic Equality in Opposition to Complexity: An Iroquoian Case Study. In *The Evolution of Political Systems: Sociopolitics in Small-Scale Sedentary Societies,* edited by Steadman Upham, pp. 119–145. Cambridge University Press, Cambridge.

Trimble, Carmen C.
1996   Paleodiet in Virginia and North Carolina as Determined by Stable Isotope Analysis of Skeletal Remains. Master's thesis, Department of Environmental Sciences, University of Virginia, Charlottesville.

Turner, Randolph E.

    1983   The Archaeological Identification of Chiefdom Societies in Southwest Virginia. In *Upland Archaeology in the East: A Symposium,* edited by Michael B. Barber, Clarence R. Geier, and George A. Tolley, pp. 271–283. Cultural Resources Report No. 2, Forest Service Southern Region. United States Department of Agriculture, Atlanta.

Tyler, Lyon (editor)

    1907   *Narratives of Early Virginia, 1600–1625.* Charles Scribner's Sons, New York.

Ubelaker, Douglas H., and Douglas W. Owsley

    2003   Isotopic Evidence for Diet in the Seventeenth-Century Colonial Chesapeake. *American Antiquity* 68(1):129–139.

Usner, Daniel H., Jr.

    1992   *Indians, Settlers, and Slaves in a Frontier Exchange Economy.* University of North Carolina Press, Chapel Hill.

Van Deelen, Timothy R., Karmen M. Hollis, Chris Anchor, and Dwayne R. Etter

    2000   Sex Affects Age Determination and Wear of Molariform Teeth in White-Tailed Deer. *Journal of Wildlife Management* 64(4):1076–1081.

Van Kirk, Sylvia

    1983   *Many Tender Ties: Women in Fur-Trade Society, 1670–1870.* University of Oklahoma Press, Norman.

Verme, Louis J.

    1969   Reproductive Patterns of White-Tailed Deer Related to Nutritional Plane. *Journal of Wildlife Management* 33(4):881–887.

Verme, Louis J., and Duane E. Ullrey

    1984   Physiology and Nutrition. In *White-Tailed Deer: Ecology and Management,* edited by Lowell K. Halls, pp. 91–118. Stackpole Books, Harrisburg, Pennsylvania.

Virginia Society of Ornithology Checklist Committee

    1979   *Virginia's Birdlife: An Annotated Checklist.* Virginia Avifauna No. 2. Virginia Society of Ornithology, Lynchburg.

Vreeland, Justin K., Duane R. Diefenbach, and Bret D. Wallingford

    2004   Survival Rates, Mortality Causes, and Habitats of Pennsylvania White-Tailed Deer Fawns. *Wildlife Society Bulletin* 32(2):542–553.

Wall, Robert, and Heather Lapham

    2003   Material Culture of the Contact Period in the Upper Potomac Valley: Chronological and Cultural Implications. *Archaeology of Eastern North America* 31:151–177.

Ward, H. Trawick

    1987   Mortuary Patterns at the Fredericks, Wall, and Mitchum Sites. In *The Siouan Project: Seasons I and II,* edited by Roy S. Dickens, Jr., H. Trawick Ward, and R. P. Stephen Davis, Jr., pp. 81–110. Monograph Series No. 1.

Research Laboratories of Anthropology, University of North Carolina, Chapel Hill.

Ward, H. Trawick, and R. P. Stephen Davis, Jr.

1993   *Indian Communities on the North Carolina Piedmont, A.D. 1000–1700.* Monograph No. 2. Research Laboratories of Anthropology, University of North Carolina, Chapel Hill.

Waselkov, Gregory A.

1977   Prehistoric Dan River Hunting Strategies. Master's thesis, Department of Anthropology, University of North Carolina, Chapel Hill.

1978   Evolution of Deer Hunting in the Eastern Woodlands. *Mid-Continental Journal of Archaeology* 3(1):15–34.

1989   Seventeenth-Century Trade in the Colonial Southeast. *Southeastern Archaeology* 8:117–133.

1993   Historic Creek Indian Responses to European Trade and the Rise of Political Factions. In *Ethnohistory and Archaeology: Approaches to Postcontact Change in the Americas,* edited by J. Daniel Rogers and Samuel M. Wilson, pp. 123–131. Plenum Press, New York.

Waselkov, Gregory A., and Kathryn E. Holland Braund (editors)

1995   *William Bartram on the Southeastern Indians.* University of Nebraska Press, Lincoln.

Wattenmaker, Patricia

1987   The Organization of Production and Consumption in a Complex Society: A Study of a Village Site in Southeast Turkey. *MASCA Journal* 4:191–203.

1998   *Household and State in Upper Mesopotamia: Specialized Economy and the Social Uses of Goods in an Early Complex Society.* Smithsonian Institution Press, Washington, D.C.

Wells, John H.

2002   *Abbyville: A Complex of Archeological Sites in John H. Kerr Reservoir, Halifax County, Virginia.* Special Publication No. 39. Archeological Society of Virginia, Richmond.

Wesson, Cameron B., and Mark A. Rees (editors)

2002   *Between Contacts and Colonies: Archaeological Perspectives on the Protohistoric Southeast.* University of Alabama Press, Tuscaloosa.

White, Bruce M.

1999   The Women Who Married a Beaver: Trade Patterns and Gender Roles in the Ojibwa Fur Trade. *Ethnohistory* 46(1):110–147.

White, Richard

1991   *The Middle Ground: Indians, Empires, and Republics in the Great Lakes Region, 1650–1815.* Cambridge University Press, Cambridge.

Whyte, Thomas R.

1999   Ichthyofaunal Remains from the Buzzard Rock Site (44RN2), Roanoke,

Virginia. Report on file with the Virginia Department of Historic Resources, Richmond.

Whyte, Thomas R., and Clarence Geier

1982   *The Perskins Point Site (44 BA3): A Protohistoric Stockaded Village on the Jackson River, Bath County, Virginia.* Occasional Papers in Anthropology No. 11. Archaeological Research Center, James Madison University, Harrisonburg.

Williams, Mark, and Gary Shapiro (editors)

1990   *Lamar Archaeology: Mississippian Chiefdoms in the Deep South.* University of Alabama Press, Tuscaloosa.

Wilson, Don E., and DeeAnn M. Reeder (editors)

1993   *Mammal Species of the World: A Taxonomic and Geographic Reference.* 2nd ed. Smithsonian Institution Press, Washington, D.C.

Wilson, Homes Hogue

1987   Human Skeletal Remains from the Wall and Fredericks Sites. In *The Siouan Project: Seasons I and II,* edited by Roy S. Dickens, Jr., H. Trawick Ward, and R. P. Stephen Davis, Jr., pp. 111–139. Monograph Series No. 1. Research Laboratories of Anthropology, University of North Carolina, Chapel Hill.

Wing, Elizabeth S., and Antoinette B. Brown

1979   *Paleonutrition: Method and Theory in Prehistoric Foodways.* Academic Press, New York.

Xie, Jialong, Harry R. Hill, Scott R. Winterstein, Henry Campa III, Robert V. Doepker, Timothy R. Van Deelen, and Jiangou Liu

1999   White-Tailed Deer Management Options Model (DeerMOM): Design, Quantification, and Application. *Ecological Modeling* 124:121–130.

Zeder, Melinda A.

1991   *Feeding Cities: Specialized Animal Economy in the Ancient Near East.* Smithsonian Institution Press, Washington, D.C.

2001   A Metrical Analysis of a Collection of Modern Goats (*Capra hircus aegargus* and *C. h. hircus)* from Iran and Iraq: Implications for the Study of Caprine Domestication. *Journal of Archaeological Science* 28:61–79.

Zeder, Melinda A., and Brian Hesse

2000   The Initial Domestication of Goats (*Capra hircus*) in the Zagros Mountains 10,000 Years Ago. *Science* 287:2254–2257.

Index

elk. *See* wapiti
England, 11
English, 2, 7, 9, 25, 94, 101, 102, 127,
  142, 144
Eno River, 103
entrepreneurs, 8, 136, 140, 141, 143
Eschelman site, 89, 101
exchange, 4, 5–6, 8, 24–25, 26, 40–41, 103,
  120, 122, 127, 132, 135, 140, 142, 144, 146
exchange, gift. *See* gift-giving

faunal analysis: analytical methods, 47–51;
  field recovery methods, 27, 28, 32, 34,
  35, 38, 52, 54, 58, 70
faunal assemblages: samples, 51–54, 124;
  summary of, 55 table 3.1; taphonomic
  biases, 33, 54–56, 57 table 3.2, 58–59, 60
  table 3.3, 61 figs. 3.1–3.2, 62, 64, 72; taxa
  identified, 62, 63 table 3.4, 64, 65–69
  table 3.5, 70–72
fishes, 21, 51, 61, 64, 72, 97; taxa identified, 70
fishhooks, 23, 96 table 4.2, 97 fig. 4.8, 98
fishing, 21
flaking tool, 96 table 4.2, 114, 116, 124
fleshing tool, 95, 96 table 4.2
Fort Ancient (Indians), 30, 44, 46
fox, 17, 64, 73–74, 75 fig. 3.5, 81; butchered
  bones, 56
French, 148
furs, 2, 5, 105, 140, 142, 144, 150; beaver, 5,
  12, 17, 73–74, 89, 142; export of, 142–43;
  export tax on, 7; fox and raccoon, 17,
  73–74; wolf, 81
fur trade, 89, 101–2, 141, 145, 148
fur traders. *See* traders

Gathright Dam, 22
gaming piece, 112
gender, 107, 139, 141, 149
generosity, 3, 137
gift-giving, 5, 6, 18, 103, 105, 111, 120, 137,
  138, 144, 147, 148
glass beads, 8, 25, 40, 89, 102, 103, 138; in
  mortuary contexts, 18, 24, 25, 105, 106,
  111, 120, 123 table 5.3, 127–28, 129 fig.
  5.11, 130–31 table 5.4, 137, 138, 146–47
gorget: copper, 125, 126 fig. 5.10, 127, 137;
  shell, 25, 26, 121 fig. 5.8, 122, 128
gouge, 96 table 4.2

Graham-White site (44RN21), 22, 23,
  25, 102
grave goods. *See* mortuary goods
Great Britain, 6, 142
guns, 7, 25, 103

hawk, 48, 64, 111, 125, 127
hawk bell, 125, 127
hearth, 29, 30, 37, 40, 52–54, 56, 62, 94
hellbender, 71–72
hematite, 124
hides. *See* deerskins
hide-working. *See* deerskin production
hide-working tools, 23, 92 fig. 4.5, 95, 96
  table 4.2, 97 fig. 4.8, 98 fig. 4.9, 99,
  101, 103, 104, 138; in mortuary contexts,
  116, 139
high-status. *See* elite
hoe, 7, 89, 95, 96 table 4.2, 149
Hoge site (44TZ6), 17, 26–27, 139; comparison of study sites, 43–44, 45 table 2.3,
  46; deer hunting and processing practices, 77, 79, 81, 82, 84, 89, 90, 91, 93–
  100, 103; mortuary data not used, 105–
  6; radiocarbon dates, 29 table 2.1, 37;
  site history, 35, 37–38; site plan, 36
  fig. 2.7; vertebrate subsistence practices,
  47, 51–54, 56, 58, 59, 62, 64, 70–74
Holland, C. G., 27, 35, 38
Holstein River, 20, 24
hunters, 10, 17–18, 42, 77, 79, 81, 82, 84,
  86, 87, 101–3, 139, 144, 149
hunting. *See* deer hunting
hunting-for-hides, 3, 9, 15, 17, 77, 101, 103
Huron (Indians), 148

infants, 107, 108, 109 table 5.1, 148; burial
  contents, 111, 113 fig. 5.2, 114, 122, 124,
  125, 128, 129; proportion buried with
  goods, 141, 145
Integrated Taxonomic Information System, 48
intensification. *See* economic intensification
iron, 25, 89, 94, 102, 103, 111

Jackson River, 22
James River, 5, 142, 143
Jamestown, 142
Jones, Emory Eugene, 35, 37